"Rusty's story is a p
pen when someone da
be better than their past. The remarkable transformation
in his own life is now making a huge impact in so many
other lives. This book will inspire you to see how God can
use all of our stories for the good."

- **Matthew West**, is a four-time GRAMMY® nominee, a multi-ple-ASCAP Christian music Songwriter/Artist of the Year winner, and a Dove Award recipient. He was awarded an American Music Award (2013), a Billboard Music Award (2014), and a K-LOVE Fan Award (2016). West also received a Primetime Emmy® Award.

"A poignant reminder that we all have 'jail cells' we allow into our lives. More importantly, *Cell 121* reminds us that we can redeem our past, make new decisions, discover the reason we were born, and make a difference in the world. An inspiring and hopeful message for anyone feeling trapped."

- **Dan Miller**, author and coach (48Days.com), and *New York Times* best-selling author.

"*Cell 121* is a raw reminder of how God's grace and love is for everyone. Rusty's life is the perfect example of how God's love can always bring hope, no matter what we may be going through. This book is guaranteed to make you laugh, make you cry, inspire you to be the person God created you to be, and leave you yearning for more of Christ's love."

- **Mike Gesell**, child of God, professional basketball player, and former starting point guard for the Iowa Hawkeyes.

"Rusty Boruff does an excellent job of transitioning the reader through a journey of their inner-self . . . surrounded by internal bars of imprisonment, to bursting free under the power of the cross of Jesus Christ! Rusty uses the storyline in *Cell 121* to guide the readers with explicit detail of how to be not just an overcomer, but to truly become MORE THAN A CONQUEROR for Jesus! *Cell 121* is a great encouragement to anyone who feels that the walls of the world are closing in and the chains of life are tightening around them!"

- **Pastor D. Robinson,** Network Director of Pastoral Care at Trinity Broadcasting Family of Networks.

"Get ready to be encouraged, empowered, and motivated. Rusty and his story is an example we all need in order to have the courage to complete our unique individual life's journey."

- **Jimmie Bell,** retired pro football player, speaker and coach, media personality, and entrepreneur.

# CELL 121

Learning to never give up on
yourself or your loved ones
in the toughest moments
of your life

RUSTY BORUFF

*I would like to dedicate this book to my beautiful wife and biggest supporter, Brook; my son, Tannen, who has changed my life and brings me so much joy; my mom and dad, Rick and Lori, who never stopped loving me and praying for me; my entire extended family including my brother and hero, Rye; and my One Eighty family.*

Please take a moment to write Rusty Boruff with any questions or thoughts on the book, or to find out more about One Eighty at:

**Rusty Boruff**
**601 Marquette Street**
**Davenport, Iowa 52802**

**Or leave a comment at www.rustyboruff.com**

The author and publisher do not intend for this book to be used as a guide to diagnose or treat medical, physiological, or psychological problems. If the reader requires expert assistance, please seek the services of your own physician or licensed counselor.

# Contents

## INTRODUCTION

**Part 1: Your Jail** .......................................... 1
We each have a jail cell. You may not be surrounded by iron bars, but if you're honest, you have your struggles, which oftentimes imprison you.

Discovering Your Jail: Facing and Identifying Your Struggles Head On

Understanding Your Jail:
Creating a Battle Plan to Fight Your Struggles

Maintaining Your Jail: Living with Struggles

**Part 2: Your Key** ......................................... 35
The crazy thing about it . . . we all have the same key.

## Overcomer. Passionate. Driven. Unstoppable.

These four words describe Rusty Boruff, a man who has been an inspiration to thousands across the world. At one time, people counted him out because he was a homeless, addicted felon, who once again found himself in cell 121. But in that cell, Rusty found the key that unlocked the emotional and spiritual bars surrounding him. And someway, somehow, he used his story as a catalyst to do what God was calling him to.

In *Cell 121* Rusty gives hope to those who have been beaten with life's circumstances, by providing practical application on how to overcome struggles.

Rusty's goal in life is simple. He wants to inspire and equip people to achieve their dreams, so that they can make an impact in their community. If this resonates with you, then you've picked up the right book.

*Cell 121* will motivate all of us to keep going. By reading this book you will be able to identify your dreams, and move closer to embodying them. It's time for you to become an overcomer—a passionate, driven, and unstoppable force that will radically change this world.

-**Kary Oberbrunner,** author of *ELIXIR Project, Day Job to Dream Job, The Deeper Path,* and *Your Secret Name.*

"My mission in life is not merely to survive, but to thrive; and to do so with some passion, some compassion, some humor, and some style."
-Maya Angelou

"When you think you have reached the end of your rope, tie a knot and hang on."
-Abraham Lincoln

"You weren't born to just live and die, you were born to make a difference."
-Rusty Boruff

# Introduction

As I rolled up my thin mat off the cold, concrete floor, I struggled to deal with the emotions of another day in jail. I'd been inside for nearly a year and potentially thirteen more, and the stress of being totally out of control took its toll on me every morning. I walked into the dayroom wearing my sandals, grabbed my bagged breakfast, and sat on the cold, steel bench.

This is what I call home. The open shower shared by twelve, the small cell where I sleep on the floor because of overcrowding, the tiny TV behind scratched glass. I never walk outside, and only receive visitors through a three-inch plastic window. For me, the worst part is the constant buzzing of the lights that remain on twenty-four/seven.

God allowed me to experience those things, but I'm grateful my story doesn't end there. After my release, I went on to start a nonprofit organization with the five hundred dollars I had in my savings account.

Today, after raising millions of dollars and creating an organization that serves thousands of people each month, God has shown me that many people are in a jail cell, even though it may not be a physical one. He showed me the key to unlock the catalyst to do what He wants us to do in our lives.

Although this book is my story, I will be sharing letters and poems one of my friends, Jeremy, wrote for his daughter, which I call *Reflections from the Other Side of Society*.[1] Jeremy is currently incarcerated and looking at life in prison, plus fifty years.

---

[1] Personal letters and poems of an inmate doing life in prison, plus fifty years, which have been edited slightly.

I've also included an **Interaction Map** at the end of each chapter with challenging questions and thoughts to create conversation and to stir your heart. This is where you as an individual, or a small group, can become interactive.

# Reflections from the Other Side of Society
## (Letter from a current inmate)

Once upon a time there was a demon-possessed man named Jeremy—and this is my story.

I went from being a proud senior in college, studying my life's passion of creative art and athletics, to my extended stay here at Scott County Jail, facing life in prison, plus fifty years. I am charged with kidnapping, arson, conspiracy, and assault charges with serious injury.

I'm the prodigal's son who has squandered family support and love for poor choice. I got involved with nearly everything in search for truth, reasoning, and purpose. I invited demons in and became addicted to drugs, especially synthetic marijuana. In between, I dropped out of college, was kicked out of my parents' house, became homeless, got my girlfriend pregnant, went broke, lost friends, and nearly lost my mind and life because of drugs.

Coming to prison brought me to my lowest point, and I cried out to God. In here, I accepted Christ as my Savior. I came in with a broken mind and God brought me mental stability. Things were so bad before I came to Jesus that when I looked into a mirror I didn't recognize myself. I wanted to crawl out of my skin. But God saved me, He saved my life. I was found guilty on all charges, and guilty before God.

My child was born on April 13, 2013, and I haven't held her yet. My fiancée left me for my best friend. I was disconnected from my family and suffered heartbreak from my bad decisions. But my future is in God's hands. *Please pray for me.*

The Lord has put it in my heart to be a father. I pray that God will not take this away because of the poor choices I have made. *"Father, please show me the way as I walk in faith. Open my heart and search my soul. Cleanse me and renew me. My sins are against You and I've felt the weight of death and pain. I've taken ahold of Your forgiveness. Father, I accept the blood of Your Son for my sins. Please show me the way. My God, show me the way. Protect my baby and have mercy on her mother. If this is what it takes to be a father, to be a man . . . Lord, here I am."*

-Jeremy

# Part 1:

Your Jail: We each have a jail cell. You may not be surrounded by iron bars, but if you're honest, you have your struggles, which oftentimes imprison you.

# 1

## Discovering Your Jail:

### Facing and Identifying Your Struggles Head On

It was the longest ride of my life. I was in the middle of nowhere in Iowa, lying in the trunk of a minivan, trying to hide my tears from the seven guys in front of me. It was the first week on my job, selling vacuum sweepers door to door. We were three hours from home when I got the call.

"Rusty, there's a warrant out for your arrest and it carries a minimum fourteen-year sentence," a somber voice said.

I remember trying to shake it off like it was nothing. Just a few days before, I found out my first kid was on the way. Then I started thinking about how my life was going to change from that one phone call. Not only would I miss my child's first word, his first touchdown, and his first hit at baseball, but I was going to have to go back to that same old dirty, cold jail cell I had just been released from a few months prior.

I had told everyone I was changing. I stopped drinking and doing drugs. I left the criminal life, and became involved in a local church. Yet just a few months out of jail on bond and I was once again faced with the reality of prison. The worst thing was knowing I would have to face all those saying, "I told you so."

Three hours in the back of this van, no one to talk to, and I tried to hide from everyone in front what would happen to me when I got home. I remember looking out the back window at the corn stalks we passed, imagining what my life was going to look like in 180 minutes.

I'd get home. Meet the cop. He'd slap on those cold, metal handcuffs I was all too familiar with, and escort me to his car, where I'd crunch into that small, secluded, lonely back seat. He'd pull into the station, they'd take all of my information, and do my beautiful portrait. I'd go into that small, dungy, yellow shower stall where I'd be strip-searched and given a black and white striped suit. Then I'd be walked to my home away from home—cell 121.

So I had to decide whether I'd run or commit suicide. In those 10,800 seconds, I made up my mind—I was gone. I couldn't handle it, couldn't disappoint once again. When we got back to the shop, I jumped in my four shades of red, beat-up car. I didn't know where I was going—just drove. Next thing I knew I was at my mentors' house, a couple from church who took me in as their son.

I completely broke down. *Fourteen years.* I'd be thirty-five before I gained my freedom. My child would be in high school, my parents aging and retired, and my brother forty. All I remember of that conversation was them praying for me and saying, "You know deep down what you have to do."

I left there that night knowing that I couldn't run, and I couldn't kill myself . . . I might miss my child's first word, first hit, and his first touchdown, but I wanted him to know his dad.

After a conversation with the local authorities, because it was so late, they agreed to let me spend my last night of freedom at my parents' house and would pick me up there in the morning. Although a blessing, it was the longest night of my life, knowing that I would wake up in the morning to a knock on the door and a man dressed in blue would take me away.

> I might miss my child's first word, first hit, and his first touchdown, but I wanted him to know his dad.

Needless to say, I didn't get much sleep. I lay awake in my twin bed, covered by a blanket my grandmother had knitted. For hours I wove my fingers in and out of the holes in the blanket, staring at the ceiling. I thought about how much I would disappoint my parents, my soon to be kid's mother, my pastor, my family, and myself. I wanted to change and I believe I did, yet here I was again, facing cell 121, and letting everyone down.

As night turned into a cold morning, the sun shone bright but felt chilly coming through the window. I lay there watching the frost melt on the glass, wishing this moment would last forever. But soon the morning frost was gone, and reality set in.

As I prepared myself to leave, Dad came to my room to say goodbye. My dad is your typical blue-collar man, hardest working guy I've ever known, and my role model. Yet he fell on his knees, wrapped his arms around my waist, and began to cry. Through his tears he murmured, "I love you."

My dad showed little emotion and had never really told me he loved me—but he always showed it with his actions. So even though I knew he loved me, hearing him say those words gave me the strength for what I heard next.

*Knock, knock, knock!* It was time.

At twenty years old, my jail cell was a physical one. But the feelings I experienced in that long ride home, that long night, and the long stay in cell 121 are the same emotions we all deal with. Because we each have our own jail cell. Sometimes we create it and other times life's circumstances happen that we have no control over. Either way, we find ourselves locked in and searching for the key.

I was tired, angry, hopeless, sad, lost, depressed, anxious, and confused, yet I knew that it was time to do something with my life.

Throughout this book you'll hear more of my story. That's one of the things we have in common, *we all have a story.* Your story may be like my wife's, who has only done three things wrong in her life, and that was when she was two years old. Or maybe your story is like mine. But the unique thing about our stories is though they may read differently, we've all faced something we can't defeat alone.

When those struggles arise, whether it be eating issues, anger, depression, addiction, self-injury, insecurities, or the darkness of death itself we have two options. In cell 121, I had a choice to make: was I going to let the time own me . . . or was I going to own the time?

One stance was defeat while the other took on victory, even if I couldn't see it when I declared it.

In order to be victorious, we must first surrender. But by human standards surrendering does not equate with victory. Today's culture tells us that to surrender is a sign of weakness, yet the Bible says that the only way to freedom is through surrender. My question for you is simple: are you strong enough to surrender or so weak that you try to resist?

The choice is yours. I want to use my story to help you walk through yours. And to bring about a voice of truth within you that says, "I can do this." You may be on that long ride home or facing that long, hopeless night, but your story doesn't end there. Your

> are you strong enough to surrender or so weak that you try to resist?

eating issue, anger, depression, addiction, self-injury, and insecurities don't define who you are. This book holds the key to the jail cell you're facing and will help you turn that struggle into the catalyst to your future and the new you.

This will also give you hope for your loved ones who are facing struggles in their life. Whenever I struggled . . . my family struggled. My family and I walked together through the journey of dealing with the pain head on. They did not enable me and allowed the consequences to become a reality.

At times, this journey will be ugly and it will be tough. But the greatest thing we can hold on to is hope.

Like many people who have struggles in their life, I didn't just wake up one day and decide to become a homeless, unruly addict.

I grew up in the typical, Illinois, blue-collar home and attended a tiny Presbyterian church. But the only God I really knew was a God of rules, telling me what I should and shouldn't do. When I couldn't live up to those standards I decided it wasn't worth it anymore. There were many events that led me to this lie, but a few stand out more than others.

We had a very well respected teacher and coach at my high school. I always felt people worshiped him for his ability to lead our school to multiple state championships. And I equated him with authority.

One day in anger, he said, "Rusty, if my kids ever grow up to be like you, I'll kill myself."

I was not a role model, just a sixteen-year-old kid. I sat there staring blankly. But when the other kids started looking at me and laughing, I felt the embarrassment turn my face a bright red. A blanket of shame covered me in that moment.

That's when I began my journey of hatred and lack of respect for those in authority. This is where my victim mentality led me down this road where I just didn't give a rip about what I did. I began believing the lie that no matter how hard I tried or what I did, it'd never be good enough. I'd always be that "black sheep of the family" or "that kid" that parents would warn their children to stay away from because, "He's trouble." That teacher's comment was always at the forefront of my thoughts and it beat me into believing those lies.

For so long I struggled with the idea that people pegged me as a criminal, someone who didn't respect those above them, and an addict, which I was. But no one ever bothered to ask, "Why is he those things?" Instead of telling me how bad I was or what I was doing was wrong I wish that someone would have simply asked me, "Why?"

I would have said, "I'm not a bad guy. I made bad decisions to fit in and to live up to a reputation, but it's not who I want to be. I don't like disappointing my parents. I hate that I'm not allowed to play sports because of my bad behavior. I've always dreamed of being an athlete in high school. You see, I didn't dream about being the bad kid and living in constant turmoil. And I don't want to be this person anymore but I honestly don't know how to stop. If I knew how, I would."

Sadly, no one ever asked me, "Why?"

Soon, being a young, rebellious kid I was suspended from school multiple times. Addiction to cocaine and the party lifestyle took over my life, and I lost all direction of who I wanted to be. Jail wasn't foreign to me—many times it was simply a temporary free night of lodging.

I don't know what you're facing today. Maybe you feel like you're in the back of that van facing the toughest moment of your life, and no one knows.

Maybe you're that dad or mom whose son or daughter is facing darkness and you'd give anything to wrap your arms around them and tell them that you love them, one more time.

You may not be facing a physical jail—maybe you are, but the emotions, feelings, and mind games are all the same. The first step in this journey is to embrace your reality—what you're dealing with is bigger than you. But have hope! There's a key to your struggle that will turn your pain into a megaphone of victory. Those battles you face today will become the catalyst to your future.

Together, we can do this.

## *Reflections from the Other Side of Society*
### (Letter from a current inmate)

Dearest Iva,

God bless you, my baby girl, and warm greetings! My fullest expression of love toward you would be a hug and kiss. I look forward to that moment every day and I have since your birth. It hurts to be separated from you in this way. Hearing you cry for the first time was bittersweet. Bitter because I couldn't be there, sweet because I heard you cry for the first time. The nurse was bathing you and I'm guessing you weren't too partial to that. But I knew you were alive and well. In that moment, I resolved fully in my heart to not give up, to keep fighting.

I haven't seen a picture of you for a few months but I hear your hair is getting longer. I can't wait to see you! I pray to God every night for your growth and protection. You really are a blessing to me, Princess, in so many ways. Hearing your voice on the phone lifts my heart from sorrow. Even if you're only crying in the background. Sometimes I like to think you're crying because I'm not there. . . .

So when I hear you, I tell myself, "I've got to get home to my baby!"

I spend all day preparing myself for that fifteen-minute phone call. I think of what I will say to you, but then I remind myself that you're just a baby. How it breaks my heart that I'm not there to pick up on your growth and see how smart you are. But I won't worry. You are in the Lord's hands and are as precious to His eyes as you are to mine. I love you, Princess, and carry you in my heart daily.

Stay strong for Daddy. Lord willing, I'll be home soon.

Love with my whole heart,

Daddy, xoxo

## Interaction Map

1. I shared the story of my dad saying he loved me and how much joy and strength that brought me. Name and explain a time where someone said something to you that brought joy and confidence to your life.

2. I shared the story of the teacher whose words affected me negatively. Share something someone has said or done to you that brought you down.

3. Can you identify your jail cell (struggle) you're facing at this time? If so, what is it?

# 2 | Understanding Your Jail:

## Creating a Battle Plan to Fight Your Struggles

I was seventeen years old, sitting at the Hardee's in my hometown, where I was fired a few years before for stealing their delicious cookies out of the freezer. But this time, I was getting ready to make one of the biggest decisions of my life: would I join the military? I was a junior in high school and trouble had already crept into my life. The majority of people thought I wanted to join the military simply because the judge thought it was the best thing for me. But I had always dreamed of being in the army, although legally, I couldn't join until my seventeenth birthday.

So here I was—my seventeenth birthday, in the middle of the Iraq and Afghanistan War, ready to sign the next four years of my life away.

I turned down the jobs with a signing bonus and took the one without the bonus—a combat life expectancy of less than twenty seconds—and became a 13 Foxtrot Forward Observer. An artillery observer must be skilled not only in fire direction, but in stealth and, if necessary, direct combat. (In the United States Army, an artillery observer is called a Fire Support Specialist but is generally known as a Forward Observer.)

**In combat situations, observers have the lowest life expectancy of any of the troops.** But my job was fairly simple: communicate battlefield intelligence such as enemy locations, strength, and activities to Command. The job was intense and lonely at times.

I was trained to go behind enemy lines and equipped to operate independently, without support for days or weeks at a time. I knew the physical demands would be rigorous since we were trained to work with the elite.

My mother was not excited about it. But at seventeen, I knew this is what I wanted to do, probably from all the John Wayne war movies my father spoon-fed me as a kid.

Between my junior and senior year of school, while all my friends were partying and chasing girls, I was at Fort Sill, Oklahoma, the hottest place on earth. And once I finished my senior year, I'd come back. My unit was finally called up, but because my older brother was in the same unit, he went, and I stayed. This was hard on me because I knew my brother wasn't excited about going. He had a fiancée, was in school, and had a good job. And here I was, just born to do this.

While enlisted, my only deployment came when I was sent to Pine Bluff, Arkansas, of all places, to be trained in nuclear, biological, and chemical warfare. Even though it was top-secret, and a cool experience, my heart was with my unit in Iraq.

At age eighteen, I got an amazing opportunity to become a private investigator. At that time, I couldn't have asked for a better job, a dream job that became a reality. I traveled the country, following and spying on people from the back of my blacked-out van, videotaping their every move. Oh, the many stories I could tell. But that job quickly came crashing down.

I was re-located to Springfield, Missouri, the Christian capital of the world. Being an introvert, the first few months I made no attempt to get to know anyone. But one nice spring day, while driving my souped-up Wrangler down Bennett Avenue, a guy pulled up next to me to compliment my Jeep. I never imagined that this conversation would lead to one of the worst relationships of my life.

This man turned into my drug dealer. After months of using cocaine, acid, pills, and other drugs, I decided to quit my private investigator job to become a full-time drug dealer.

Obviously, this didn't work. By the age of nineteen, I was homeless. I sold everything I had, including my soul, for an empty life of drugs and alcohol.

One day I woke up in the back of a van feeling hopeless, worse than I'd ever felt in my life. So I broke into hotel rooms to have a safe and warm place to stay.

Eventually, I knew I had to get out of the area, even though I knew it meant leaving the last of my personal property behind. I wasn't ready to leave my lifestyle, however, I knew deep down that I couldn't continue living the way I was.

But I didn't have the accountability and personal discipline to quit my addictions. No matter how far or hard I ran from my surroundings, I couldn't shake the struggles I was facing. It was like I was bitten by the Devil and it was affecting my physical body and mind. The worst thing was that at that time I had no idea what the cure was.

This curse followed me back to my hometown, where I ignorantly thought a change of scenery would be what I needed. But once again, I was a homeless bum going from place to place.

Eventually, this lifestyle caught up to me when I wanted to take a girl on a date to see a movie. But with no money, I had nothing with which to feed my drug addiction. So I broke into the house next door to where I was staying, in broad daylight, and stole everything I could get my hands on.

I pawned the items and used that money to take the girl on a date. Later that evening, I watched from the porch while the cops interviewed the family I'd robbed. I walked over, looked the owners and cops in the eye, and offered to help in any way possible. That's how sick my mind was at that time.

That day, I threw away years of hard work as a private investigator. Due to my addiction, I made many sick and bad decisions and my dream job vanished in just a few moments.

Although they had no evidence, the authorities knew I'd done the burglary. But I was so tired of running, of lying and manipulating people, and just tired of living like that. I knew I had to make a drastic change in my life. So I made the short trip to the police station and turned myself in.

To be honest, I don't remember much of what happened after that. I only served a few months before my parents bailed me out of jail.

However, I do remember that this was the first time I really faced my bad decisions. Due to my incarceration, I was "less than honorably discharged" from the military. And once again, my own horrible decisions had stripped away one of my dreams. I learned the hard way that as you go about developing and preparing your dreams, every decision you make drastically impacts you actually living it.

After my release, I spent the next few months starting to engage in church, going through recovery programs, and tried my hardest to find new and healthy friends.

I finally got a job selling Kirby vacuums and I was back on track with my life.

But suddenly, my entire world took a turn for the worse. I received that phone call I mentioned in the beginning. First, the call. Second, the longest ride of my life. Third, the longest night of my life. There's no question that I was trying to change who I was for the better, but once again, I found myself locked up. This time it was even more serious.

Here I was, sitting in this eight by eight room on a cold, steel chair. Only a small wooden table separated me from two detectives. When I sat down I didn't realize that this would be one of the most important moments of my life.

One of the detectives looked straight into my eyes, and said, "You're already facing multiple theft and burglary counts. We're working on a drug conspiracy charge for carrying over half a million dollars worth of drugs over state borders in the last six months. And I'm here to tell you that we're charging you with over thirty counts of criminal sexual assault. Don't be surprised if you spend the next forty years sitting in an Illinois prison."

I was twenty years old and was intimate with my sixteen-year-old girlfriend. We weren't hiding our relationship, both our parents knew, and it was public knowledge. But I was the rebel kid and she was the high school cheerleader. By this time, word had spread that she was pregnant with my soon-to-be child. Even though her parents weren't pressing charges the state attorney decided to charge me with each alleged time we had sexual contact.

I want to clarify here that these charges were later dropped to a misdemeanor battery charge and I didn't have to register on the Sex Offender Registry. But for seven months the words, "You are a criminal sex offender," never left me.

While sitting in cell 121, reality settled in when I read in the newspaper how I was such a horrible person. I remember lying in my three-man cell, where I slept on the floor due to overcrowding, and saying out loud; "I'm not who they say I am. I'm just a dumb kid." But the overwhelming pressure of public opinion, the stress of being in jail with my destiny and future lying in the fate of another person, and the anxiety of having a son I may never see was overwhelming.

I felt like I deserved whatever sentence was handed down on the drug charges and burglary, since I knew I'd done something horribly wrong there. But I tried to justify my actions, saying, "I'm not a sexual predator," which I was being labeled. "I'm simply a teenager with hormones who was in love with a girl four years younger than me."

No matter how much I justified it in my mind, no matter how much I thought, worried, and stressed over it, the words from that detective still rang through my head.

The crazy thing is that I wouldn't change his words even if I could. Because it was those words that led me to the key that unlocked my jail cell. No, it didn't unlock the physical jail that I was in. But it unlocked the spiritual and emotional jail I found myself in, which was much worse than the physical jail.

The key for me—Jesus Christ! Before, Jesus was just some magical character that my mom preached about all the time. I'd come home from partying all night to find some book about this Jesus dude lying on my pillow and

I simply threw it in the pile with the rest of the books she left for me after a long night.

But for the first time in my life, Jesus became more than just an annoying character. I found myself in a situation where I literally had no other option than to rely on Him. I couldn't go another day with the stress, worry, anger, heartbreak, anxiety, and depression. But everywhere I looked . . . there He was. Even on TV, one of the only channels we got was TBN (Trinity Broadcasting Network).

I had tried the God thing before when I was in jail and even for a short time in the military, but though my heart was right . . . it just wasn't real to me. *But this time was different.*

> **I found myself in a situation where I literally had no other option than to rely on Him.**

One cold, lonely night, I told God, *"I'm completely done with my old life. I realize that You have been there for me the whole time. I just wasn't paying attention. You had to place me in such a desperate situation that it would get my attention—cell 121."*

And just like in my life, there has never been a situation or experience in *your* life that God didn't get you through, even if you didn't realize it at the time.

I'm thankful that in the hardest moment of my life, I discovered my key. What I found out during the past few years is that this key works in every arena of my life. The question is whether I'll pick up the key, put it in the lock, and turn it.

In order for me to understand that there was a different way to live my life, I first had to find hope. This hope came from a gentleman named Merle. He and another volunteer named Jim, both Christians, visited inmates at the Mercer County Jail and they visited me. Merle will never know how big an impact he made on my life. This 5 foot 4, 119-pound inmate was always the first in his class. Merle wasn't the most exciting speaker in the world; he would actually fall asleep while talking to us sometimes. But it was never what Merle said that really made a difference, it's what he did.

Because Merle showed up at that jail every week, I realized that God could forgive a screw-up like me. It also showed me that someone believed in me. No matter what I had done and the people I'd hurt, there was someone beyond my family who believed in Rusty Lee Boruff.

Merle was the physical start of my life-changing experience. He was my very own Billy Graham, and he ushered me into a new-found hope. This eighty-year-old man walked into the same jail week in and week out, forging ahead no matter the weather, and he wasn't afraid to go where most would fear to tread. Merle took that dark and depressed place and turned it into a sanctuary.

It doesn't matter who you are, who your parents are, or your bankroll. We all experience those dark and depressed places—they just look different for each of us.

The fact is, in those moments, we all need a Merle.

Merle realized a key in life that took me years to learn: *There is more to life than just the mistakes a person has made.* For a long time, I didn't feel like I could have an encounter with forgiveness and grace. But I eventually learned that God made man from dust, and if He could do that . . . surely He could make a new person out of my mess.

> There is more to life than just the mistakes a person has made.

One of the many things I learned in my military service was, you have to have a battle plan. I knew that in order for God to do something with my life, I had to be proactive and create that plan. Thankfully, I had experience in making plans like this because as a 13 Foxtrot Forward Observer my job was to map out enemy and friendly lines. I tracked the movements and made a battle plan.

I don't count the time I was enlisted as a waste, mostly because I had the honor of serving my country. But I also learned many valuable lessons that didn't just apply to wearing a uniform in the United States Army. While sitting in cell 121, I knew I had to do the same thing in there as when I was in the military.

When I created a battle plan as a 13 Foxtrot, I first had to map out the enemy position, and so I had to do the same for my life. But in order to identify the enemy and build a battle plan I had to be completely honest with myself.

My first step in transforming myself was choosing what I desired. After all, how many things in life do you pursue if you don't first really want them? None. If you want to stop worrying—choose not to worry. How you see that out is the next step.

If you want to stop drinking, gambling, eating unhealthy foods, self-injuring, or living in depression or anxiety then I encourage you to develop a hate for those things. Until I learned to hate cocaine and the affects it had in my life I knew I'd always want to do it, and that desire moved me to choose cocaine time after time.

Oftentimes people don't choose to create a battle plan to fight the reality of their struggles because it takes guts. It takes risk. Think of the story in the Bible when Peter walked on water over to Jesus (see Matthew 14:27–29). He never would have walked on the water if he didn't first have the guts to take the risk and step out of that boat.

Stop and think about that for a minute, then I challenge you to step out of your boat, step out of your comfort zone and take a risk. It's well worth it.

After you choose what you really desire, and are willing to risk everything for it, then you must become truly desperate to obtain it.

My moment of true desperation came in the form of my sentencing day. I was sitting in front of the judge with my attorney next to me. Seated at the table to my left, about six feet away, was the state attorney and his assistant. Behind us was a packed courtroom filled with friends and family waiting to see what my sentence would be. My attorney was hoping for four years, but we knew the state wanted fourteen.

I was wearing black and white stripes, my hands cuffed together, and my legs were shackled. A leather belt was around my waist, clipping the chains from my legs and hands together. I was worried. I knew the fate of the next decade of my life was going to be handed to me by a judge who knew nothing about me besides what he read in the small town paper.

Next thing I know, in the middle of my sentencing, a lady, whom I faintly recognized as a friend of my soon-to-be-baby's mother, bursts into the courtroom, and yells, "It's a boy!" I knew immediately that in just a few months I would be having a son.

That should have been one of the happiest moments in my life, but it quickly turned into the saddest. I couldn't turn around and hug my parents, instead I had to just sit there in those cold, metal chains. Yet thoughts of my having a boy swirled around in my fogged mind. *Who is going to coach my boy in baseball? Who's going to teach him to do a lay-up? I won't be there when he gets a crush on a girl in his class—I won't be there for him to talk to.*

With my back turned, my friends and family couldn't see the cold tears drop down my cheeks, only the judge sitting in front of me could.

Reality finally hit me like a load of bricks. My life and all my decisions, past and future, were going to impact not just me, but my son too. *All the decisions I make will change the course of history in my family's lives and it will impact eternity.*

I was already on an emotional roller coaster that day in the courtroom and now I just found out that I was going to be having a son. Anxiety, anger, joy, and pain all at once flowed over me, but nothing could prepare me for what was about to happen.

> **With my back turned, my friends and family couldn't see the cold tears drop down my cheeks, only the judge sitting in front of me could.**

That judge, who in the past had never been too fond of me, began to speak. He told the packed courtroom, "The state's initial reports asked for a sentence of fourteen years." The judge paused and looked straight at me. "However, I felt that was extreme, so now they're asking for a minimum of four years in prison." He looked at my lawyer, then back at me. "Your attorney has asked for a year of boot camp."

I knew it was a warm, sunny day, but I felt cold all over. I hardly dared to breathe as I stared at the judge.

"Rusty Lee Boruff, I've taken everything into consideration and I sentence you to seventy-five more days in county jail. You will also pay the court fines, and I will extend your probationary period to four years. However, you will not have to register as a Sex Offender. Court is adjourned."

I felt as though I'd just fallen off the top of a tall building and instead of lying crushed in the street, I had landed on a soft mattress. Tears of joy filled my eyes and ran down my face. I was so happy knowing that I'd be released in seventy-five days and no prison. But in that moment, I also knew that I was completely done with my old life.

Sometimes we have to be in the most desperate place of our life before we'll reach out to God for His help.

We see an example of this in Luke 8:40–48, the story of the woman who bled for twelve years. She'd spent everything she had on doctors, none of whom could help her. She was considered ceremonially unclean, so she was separated from society, couldn't get married, and wasn't allowed to touch anyone. But this woman was so desperate for God that she fought her way through the crowd and touched just the fringe on Jesus' robe.

In today's world, think of her as someone walking around New York City covered in anthrax, and running up to the president of the United States and giving him a hug. But this woman in the Bible did it because she desperately desired change.

I and that woman two thousand years ago had something in common that afternoon—we hated who we had become, were desperate for change, and were ready to risk everything to make the necessary revisions in life. That day was the first time I can recall truly hating all of the things in my life that led me to that wooden chair in front of that gray-haired judge.

The battle plan of changing my life, accompanied by the risk of following it out, led to the ability to achieve my desire of revising who I had become. Won't you take these steps today and become the person you most desire to be?

## *Reflections from the Other Side of Society*
(Poem from a current inmate)

**Perpetual Choices**

We are perpetually perplexed into motion. Dumbfounded
we find a reason to keep going. No gratitude do we show,
oblivious to the fact we have obtained something unstained
by the love that we lack. If we light ourselves on fire, people
will watch us burn. Be careful what you wish for 'cause we
get what we deserve. We distraughtly throw in the towel,
tired of reaping what we sowed. We paddle frantically on
a boat that won't float. Our own will becomes taxing to
the overworked mind. Tiptoeing on these eggshells while
the clock ticks of time. The present is a gift. If I accept it,
I am free. But we struggle to about-face and put flight to
these feet. So easily we alleviate temporarily with relief,
but so quickly we are tempted by the whispers of the best.
We are blessed with a choice and a chance to understand.
You can burn with the masses or take God by His hand.

## Interaction Map

1. Share a story of an opportunity that you squandered away due to bad decisions. Was it a relationship with a loved one, a job, finances, or something else?

2. Who in your life is giving you hope, and to whom can you look to for hope? Explain.

3. List one or two steps in your "battle plan."

4. Looking back at your "jail" that you identified in chapter 1, explain how desperate you are, and what that desperation means to you.

# 3

# Understanding Your Jail:

## Maintaining Your Jail: Living with Struggles

Cell 121 became a training ground for what God was calling me to do. After years of living, maintaining, and fighting with my challenges in life, I went on to start a nonprofit organization, which I'll tell you more about later in the book. However, in order to make the change from a jail cell to running a nonprofit, I had to get real about fighting the struggles I would face each day—and still battle today. I wish I could tell you that all I had to do was "desire" to change my life and it happened. In reality, it's much more complicated than that.

What I have come to believe and understand is that we are who we are because we think the way we think, which causes us to do the things we do. In other words, most of us live a life that is driven by our emotions, fears, desires, and feelings, and the life we live is in reverse of what we are supposed to.

The beginning of wisdom is recognizing what you don't know. My pastor taught me that God does not consult your past in order to determine your future. Take comfort in knowing that if you want to change—you can!

Thinking is like wearing colored sunglasses. We get so used to them that we forget we have them on, yet those glasses make everything look a certain way. If they're dark glasses, things appear darker. Whatever color your lenses are, everything you see becomes that color.

The same thing goes for if you think "me, me, me," you'll act like "me, me, me," because the way we think determines the way we act. Proverbs 23:7 says, "As a man thinks in his heart so is he" (KJV).

Patterns of thinking aren't given to us, they're learned, therefore, it takes time to unlearn these habits and belief systems. You can't see thinking—it's invisible, but its effects are powerful.

Two people facing the same situation will respond in different ways. One person may end up hurting someone; the other may save someone's life. The difference in how they react is in how they think.

Most of us have experienced so much hurt in our lives. But it's what you do with that hurt and pain that makes the difference. Don't use the sorrow, pain, guilt, and hurt as an excuse to go back to your old ways. Instead use them as a reminder of the torment that your old lifestyle brought you.

Usually the hardest thing to do in life is the right thing. And the way you think determines how you act. You can spend your whole life trying to fix the way you act, but if you never change the way you think, it won't do you any good.

> Usually the hardest thing to do in life is the right thing.

A battle plan starts with the desire to make the plan, followed by the risk of doing what it takes to create it (although your thoughts often keep you from implementing it). There's no secret hack you can use to change your thought pattern, just first, recognize that your thoughts are a hindrance, then do what Romans 12:2 says—renew your mind.

I can't create your battle plan for you, only you can. But mine is fairly simple: I surround myself with accountability and community. And I stay close to my Creator, Jesus Christ, through reading His Word and praying. My battle plan is nothing without those pillars.

For your battle plan to succeed you have to be willing to go back and repair the foundations of your life. Just like in construction where you have to repair the foundation of a building due to weathering, so in your life you must repair the foundation due to the storms you have endured.

As humans, we have a tendency to lie to ourselves when we see a commercial on TV, a billboard advertisement, or hear a preacher talk about "If you do xxx, your life will change!" But you won't hear that from me in this chapter. I do believe God can deliver people from struggles in their life—He's done it in my life and can do it in yours. But the reality is sometimes, like Paul in the Bible, you will have a "thorn in your side" (see 2 Corinthians 12:7–10).

I've watched as people have gone through programs in their life, oftentimes going to over a dozen treatment centers. At some of these places they're told, "If you just hand over your struggles to God (or your higher power), they will all go away." But when that temptation hits . . . . they relapse . . . and they're left thinking God isn't real because this happened to them, or they think something is wrong with them. The fact is, everyone struggles with something in life. And if you're honest, there's something you're struggling with today that you haven't been able to beat: lust, food, anger, depression, or something else.

I can now honestly say that I no longer struggle to remain clean and sober. But that doesn't mean I don't struggle. Every day I have to work at keeping God at the center of my life and not my job. Not only that, I have to fight to remain pure in my motives and thoughts.

This is where *grace* comes in. Grace isn't something we deserve, but it's something we're given as Christians. At the same time, grace is not an excuse to sin.

No one will be perfect in this life. But think about this, God would rather you run hard after Him and fall, than not run at all. If you never try, you'll never stand a chance. But if you try and fall, well, pick yourself up and try again. Just because you try to turn your life around, doesn't mean the scenery will change immediately. And that's okay.

> God would rather you run hard after Him and fall, than not run at all.

Have you ever driven down the road and on one side it looks like a storm is rolling in, with dark skies, rain, and maybe some lightning, while on the other side it's sunny and eighty degrees? That's life. What makes the difference between storm or sun is the window you decide to look through. Life is that car you're steering, and the direction and destination never changes—the view does. And 99 percent of the problems we face in life are because of our perspective.

So you've discovered your jail cell, and you created a plan. That's good and you're doing great, but sadly, that's not the end of the story, because two things will come and try to rob you of your joy: conflict and crisis.

Conflict will happen—in your business, your ministry, your family, and in your life. The question is, what will you do with it? Conflict in itself doesn't have the power to change a situation. But how you handle it, does.

I've learned that in conflict my enemy is no longer my foe if I turn them into my friend. Oftentimes while in conflict I became defensive. But when I started to defend myself is when the battle began. In conflict, once my point is made, it's important for me to back off, even when I don't want to. I learned not to drop a bomb when a slingshot will work. And many times I had the right words but not the right attitude. If you're looking forward to conflict and setting someone straight, I can guarantee that you aren't ready to address it yet.

Then there's crisis. When crisis hits, and it will, just remember that a crisis is simply God's alarm clock. It's the instance that pushes you to the miracle moment in your life. Those crisis situations often bring you to your knees, humble you, and take you to a point where you have no other option than to rely on someone much bigger than you: God.

Crisis is directly related to dependency. I've only been involved in vocational ministry for seven years. But within those few years, I've noticed something that larger organizations and churches have in common. A lack of dependency on God. It's never done intentionally, but subconsciously it becomes reality. When you don't know how you'll pay your bills, when your marriage is on the rocks, when you struggle every day to not pick up that bottle or pill, that's when you have a clear opportunity to become 100 percent dependent on God, which is exactly where He wants you.

But as a human, you lie to yourself by thinking you've done such a great job of growing your business, church, ministry, or life that you don't need anything else. Or that your bank account or your wisdom will get you through. And it might. But sadly, that dependency that can't usually be seen by the naked eye, handicaps your faith and you become dependent only on what you see with your human eyes.

Once you start putting your battle plan into action, it'll be easy to quit when a crisis or conflict arises. However, you must always have God's grace at the forefront of your mind and be willing to evaluate your thinking. In order to gain victory in your life, you don't have to live perfectly, never making a mistake. You simply have to be humble enough to get in the fight, recognize your weaknesses, and work on renewing your mind. This formula creates dependency on God and only then can you truly find victory.

# Reflections from the Other Side of Society
### (Letter from a current inmate)

Iva,

Hey love, what's going on? If you could respond, you would probably say, "Not much Da-da, just doing baby things that babies do." And you might say, "When are you coming home? I can't wait to have you hug me and love me for the first time!" But of course you can't speak or write yet.

I just recently had to make a hard decision. But you hold the centerpiece of my heart and you are the reason I am still fighting.

But more painfully, I've had to let you go. In order to do that I had to give you over to God. Basically, it means entrusting your very life, protection, and care to Him.

At that moment of letting go, I realized that I can't do those things for you. I'm also doing this because my intention is to put God at the forefront of my life. I've got to fully recognize who is in control. It hasn't been easy because in letting go, there's also been a deep fear that I'm missing out on too much of your life. I love you.

Daddy

**Interaction Map**

1. Rate how healthy your thinking is on a scale of one to ten, with ten being the healthiest. Explain why.

2. How does conflict and crisis get in the way of you breaking out of your jail cell?

3. Discuss something you're facing in your life today that has been or could be a lifelong battle.

# Part 2:

Your Key: The crazy thing about it . . . we all have the same key.

# 4

# Discovering Your Key:

## Tapping into the Power that Sets You Free

Your first step here is to realize that there is a key. To be honest, this takes being in a situation where you realize you actually need a key. Most of us think this thing called *life* is under control. Until one day, out of nowhere (you think), you're sitting in a jail cell, under a bridge, in a hospital, or some other tragic event happens in your life. But even though the first step seems simple, it's actually the hardest.

It's so easy to believe the lie that just because you have a good job or are a leader in your church, that nothing can harm you. But in a moment, your American Dream comfort can vanish. In Matthew 11, God says His yoke is easy and His burden is light. In life though, you yoke yourself to your kids, your job, your title, your bank account . . . so when your kids don't live up to the family name, you're fired from your job, you don't get the promotion, or you come into financial trouble, it feels as if your entire life is coming to an end. You've yoked yourself to things whose burden is heavy instead of yoking yourself to Christ whose burden is light.

The second step in this chapter is to put the key into the lock. And it takes guts to change. In jail there were times when I was ridiculed, told I just had jail-house Christianity, and that I was an idiot for even trying this Jesus thing. But this was my action step of unlocking my jail cell.

While locked up, a guy in the cell next to mine tried to escape by digging his way out with a spoon. Bro, let me tell you, the wall is six feet thick and behind that is another six-foot-thick wall. A spoon won't do the job. But how many of us try something like that when we want to escape the harsh reality of our situation? We pick up the spoon and ignore the key lying next to us.

Once I realized I needed my key, and committed myself to pick it up, the next step was putting the thing to use. I couldn't just talk about it anymore. I actually had to do something with it. Trust me, there were times when I put it in the lock . . . then took a step back. I told people that I was doing this Jesus thing, but I had a tough time living out what I said I was doing.

But do you want to know something awesome? Once I started telling people that I was a follower of Christ, I used their judgment and ridicule to hold me accountable so I could use the key and turn it. I used their disbelief as a spark to light the fire of motivation to see this thing out.

Jesus (the key), doesn't just unlock major things in life. He also works within our daily struggles as humans. I was reminded of this a few years back.

I love Jeep Wranglers, I've had them all my life until about five years ago. My wife and I moved into our first apartment together a few years back and one of the first things I noticed was our next door neighbors had a Jeep Wrangler. I was so jealous. I'd look out my apartment window and see the Jeep. I drove by their house at least twice a day, usually more, just to see that Jeep. Each time, this desire to get a Jeep became almost unbearable!

Finally one 4th of July, I broke down, drove seven hours, and bought myself a Jeep Wrangler. After the long trek home, I drove by my neighbors' house, prepared to show off my beautiful new Jeep. But then I noticed something about my neighbors' Jeep—it was actually a Humvee. I'd thought I was very observant and a smart guy—until that moment.

Never before in all those years of driving by my neighbors' day after day, did I ever realize that it wasn't a Jeep. Even to this day I think, *How could I have not noticed that?* I've owned half a dozen Wranglers and spent day after day looking at them. So I'm confident that God used that as a teaching moment for me. Keeping up with the Joneses never works. While God delivered me from the addiction of cocaine and other substances, things such as greed often still have their way with me.

Everyone wants to think, "I've got my stuff together," but in reality, we all struggle with something. And some people are stuck living in the past.

There was a time in my life when I spent five nights a week, at five different churches, attending recovery meetings. I finally realized that God had delivered me from my addiction to drugs and alcohol . . . so did I really need to be investing so much time into "recovering" from them?

God doesn't look back at the things you've done in your life and think about how bad a person you are. So why do you? Once God has forgiven you for your past, He

> God doesn't look back at the things you've done in your life and think about how bad a person you are. So why do you?

forgets it happened. If He's already forgiven you, who are you to not forgive yourself by hanging on to your past?

In order to tap into that power that sets us free, it's vital that we are dependent on the One who gives us breath. In the beginning of my ministry, while in my early twenties, I learned what it meant to be dependent on God.

After I was released from jail it was difficult finding work. Let's be honest, a felon, fresh out of jail, isn't a sexy hire. But finally, a company called Riddell Roofing gave me a shot. I worked there for a few years, earned better pay, gained their trust, and to be honest, I could have easily made a career as a welder for commercial roofs. But I knew that wasn't what I was created to do.

One beautiful day, I was standing on a roof by myself, just looking up to the sky, and I knew that God was calling me to something different. At that moment, I made the decision to become 100 percent dependent upon God. Through a series of events, which I'll explain later, I set out to build what God had placed in my heart while in cell 121: a home for men when they got out of jail.

Everything was set to launch in January, 2009. But in late 2008, I realized I still had plenty of groundwork to do. I had to figure out how to raise the $12,000 budget I had for that first year. You have to understand, I couldn't just ask my family for the money. My parents were not wealthy, just hard-working, blue-collar folks, and money was tight. I grew up eating bologna sandwiches, sometimes three times a day.

I started sending out support letters and got a few hundred dollars back in the fall. And with a few hundred dollars from my savings, I still had eleven thousand dollars to go. Someone loaned me a small office, but it was forty-five minutes away from where I called home in Aledo, Illinois. So for three months, I drove the forty-five minutes to the office where I tried to figure out how to raise the rest of the money.

There were nights where, honest to God, I didn't have a dime left, and my office often became my bedroom. Because I didn't want people to know I didn't have enough gas to make the trip back and forth, I parked down the road, brought in a change of clothes, and slept under my desk. Even though it was a season full of struggle, it was one my best because I was 100 percent dependent upon God.

The first two years of ministry, 2009 and 2010, were tough. In 2010, I struggled to raise the money to keep the doors open, knowing I had ten guys who were depending on me to keep One Eighty open. So I worked a second job as a roofer. I told people I was doing it because I needed to "get away" and it was my escape.

That first year, I raised $6,500, and the other $5,500 came from my second job. The struggle of working two jobs wasn't fun or easy, but it was one of the sweetest and most peaceful seasons of my life because I was depending upon God—100 percent.

Due to the weather in late 2010, I could no longer roof, so I had to supplement the income somehow. If you do the math, including my pay, a $12,000 budget wasn't really very much. I found an online ad for work with flexible hours at $10 an hour. The only catch, it was shoveling manure at a horse farm. But since I'd grown up training horses, I saw it as an easy sell to anyone who might question why I was doing it.

So for three hours every day, I'd go shovel crap. I was ashamed to let most people know, so once again, I did my best to hide it. However, I told those who found out that I loved horses, which I did, just not their crap.

When I reflect on those moments in my life, I realize they were some of the best—I was dependent on God—*and He never let me down.*

A while back, someone asked me, "When you're living with an addiction (which is a disease), what's the most important thing to do?"

My answer was simple. "Know that you cannot be dependent on anyone besides the One who created you."

When it comes to your struggles, or the faith to do something radical in your life, the only way to truly maintain your struggles and live with them, is to be completely dependent upon God to get you through them. Just like the early days in ministry when I had no other option but to be 100 percent dependent upon Him.

Often, once you discover the key and unlock your jail, you think you have your life under control. But what you're really doing is replacing the old jail cell with a new one. Once you unlock the door to your house, do you then throw away the key? Of course not, because you'll need it again. Today, I still have to keep reusing the key that brings freedom, healing, and peace.

Sunday is the worst day of the week for me. I hate that day. I know that sounds crazy, but let me explain. My son, Tannen, lives in my hometown, about forty minutes from my wife and I, and his mother has full custody. She and I have a good relationship so even though my wife and I could get joint custody, there just hasn't been any reason. I'm married to a beautiful, amazing woman, Brook. And Brook and I have Tannen every weekend and usually see him once during the week.

This is how Sunday looks for us. We get up, get ready to go to church, attend church as a family, go to my in-laws' for a family lunch, hang out for a few hours, and then I take Tannen home. But that forty-minute drive to his house is the worst forty minutes of my week. I drop him off, knowing I may not see him again until the next weekend, which hurts me more than you can imagine.

My job, on a day-to-day basis, has a high level of stress. Running a nonprofit, raising millions of dollars, leading hundreds of staff and volunteers, working with returning citizens (inmates), and dealing with kids who live in poverty can make for some very tough moments throughout the week. But nothing compares to that forty-minute drive where I know at the end I'm going to have to say, "I love you, buddy. I'm going to miss you."

That's why I hate Sundays.

But once again, the same Jesus that was my key in cell 121, is the same Jesus that's my key to getting through my tough moments today.

> But nothing compares to that forty-minute drive where I know at the end I'm going to have to say, "I love you, buddy. I'm going to miss you."

My mom's mother (Grandma) is a beautiful woman inside and out. She's also a magnificent piano player. As I child, I used to go over to her house and she taught me how to play the piano. Even though I never got the hang of it, I'll never forget the days sitting in front of that piano, eating vanilla wafers, and plugging away on that instrument in her living room overlooking a beautiful lake.

One of the songs I practiced had lyrics that said, "He's (God) got the whole world in His hands, He's got the whole wide world, in His hands."[2] I never thought that twenty years later, on that long ride taking my son home

---

[2] He's God the Whole World in His Hands, in public domain.

for the week, the memories of that song would get me through the heartache and pain I feel every Sunday. I've learned that I have no other option but to trust in Him, and that He really does have the whole world in His hands, even that situation.

Tapping into the power that sets us free from worry, guilt, anger, depression, and anxiety can only be done if it's drawn from a dependency on God. And realizing that if God has the whole world in His hands, then He can handle every situation that we find ourselves in, no matter how big or small.

## Reflections from the Other Side of Society
(Poems from a current inmate)

### Metamorphosis

I can see how it would be hard to understand the love of another. So deep it moves the angels to dance. It's hard-wired in our brain to be skeptical to the fact that the Father sent His Son to die at human hands. Through demonic ways the masochist raged. No light to be seen. The colors fade to fifty shades of gray. We externalize our shame until the finger points to another we can blame. On the edge, and all it takes is a shift of fate in the wrong direction, causing catastrophic events to emerge from the ashes. A collision of parallel circumstances dances in and is hidden behind the stare of a pair of eyelashes. And with the world crashing down around you, cause and effect, a voice to resonate and abound to . . . the heavens, I'll speak clearly so you can hear the message, brethren. We can just be a paradox of predictions or chance matter meeting like Darwin envisioned. This is a metamorphosis, metaphorically speaking, bringing the vision to light so you can stop dreaming. Not just a flash in the pan for the excitement of the masses, but a beacon of hope for the seekers of passion.

### The Message

We find ourselves under the influence of our own design. Owners of land deeds of dead men where our feet reside. Shaky ground becomes expansive, transparency achieved by the masses. Corrupt thoughts will run rampant, left unattended, they hinder our passion and obscure our path to a life everlasting. Washed in the blood, we are blessed with a promise of peace, our soul can rest, through the water we gain respect for God's love, and in retrospect, we are loved because we are one. We emerge from the scum and the mud, made brand new because of His love, through His grace we stood back up. We became one in an emission of molecules split from the hairs of Adam's follicles, which following us is a gravitational pull. Like the gospel Word it is spreading, on the earth His Spirit is descending. The concept of love, the Lord is avenging, the request to come home, His hand is extending, urging the thief to give back what he stole. Robbing the holy land of the virtuous souls. Well, cork this message in a bottle and send it with faith that it will transcend what we know of time and of space.

## Interaction Map

1. Share an example of someone, maybe even yourself, that on the outside looks like they have it all together, but in reality, they need the key just like anyone else.

2. For me, the key was Jesus. Who or what do you identify as the key? And why?

3. Are you dependent on God or yourself? Why?

4. Do you believe the key can unlock other jail cells in your life that you may find yourself in? If so, what are they?

# 5 | Understanding Your Key:

## How to Use that Same Key in Other Areas of Life

Early in 2016, One Eighty, the organization I have the honor to lead, decided we would purchase some properties in the heart of Davenport, Iowa. This wasn't just a house or two. It was literally an entire city block. It included multiple homes, empty lots, abandoned school, offices, church, and other out buildings. It would be a multi-million-dollar project. It was once a thriving area that had been ravaged by homelessness, poverty, and addiction over the past thirty years. For about six months, it felt like we were on a roller coaster working up to these properties.

It wasn't a surprise to me that it was going to be a battle. A few years earlier, One Eighty expanded our men's residential program—we decided to explore the notion of moving it into a more rural setting versus being smack dab in the middle of town. You have to understand, in America we have something called, "Not in My Backyard Syndrome." Everyone loves the idea of people changing their lives—just don't do it in *my* backyard. Which, as a father and a past addict, I understand and have sympathy for, but if no one is willing to have it in their backyard ... then we have an issue.

Thankfully, the United States government understood this back in the 1980's, and saw it was presenting an issue to those who truly wanted to change. So they created the Americans with Disabilities Act and the Federal Fair Housing Act. Both of these protect organizations like us, and protect our residents' right to affordable and safe housing.

We felt moving out into the country where we only had a few neighbors would be smart. Less of a chance of people becoming upset.

Wrong.

Within a few weeks, I found myself at the county council meetings dealing with a large group of protesters—some our neighbors, others just people who apparently don't like the idea of who we are. The meetings got so heated that eventually I was assigned security to usher me in and out. After a long battle, thankfully, the law was upheld and we were allowed to stay there.

But this wasn't my first time dealing with this issue. Just a year before that, we opened up a facility for mothers and kids who were homeless. Great idea, right? Not according to the city and specifically one alderman who absolutely had it out for us. Come to find out, it wasn't so much what we were trying to do but who we were that upset him—the idea that a Christian organization was doing this work, when he thought it should be the government's responsibility. Of course, as a Christian, I see it the other way around.

The battle over opening these properties grew intense and was fought over the front pages of major newspapers in the area and in people's homes via their TV screens.

Once again though, the fight for justice was worth it because the law was upheld.

So in 2016, I was prepared to deal with anything that came my way. We moved forward with the purchase of a city block, which would be transformed to revive a hurting community. By this time, I had plenty of experience with things such as the city, county, and real estate transactions.

But this one was like no other. It was complicated, confusing, and at times a nightmare. But deep down, we knew this was where God wanted us and that the Enemy wasn't happy with what we were going to be using it for.

Because the lease on one of our other properties was expiring we were under a strict timeline on this new one. It felt like everything hinged on this massive real estate transaction. The weight of this deal—the stress and pressure—was like no other. If we didn't close on this property, what would we do with a house full of broken women who were trying to change their life? We also had multiple major events and campaigns hanging on this transaction. People were excited and thousands of dollars had already been spent to make it happen.

Only my attorney and I knew that on Monday, April 25, 2016, when I walked into my lawyer's office, there was a high chance this deal wouldn't happen.

Now to save you from the suspense—it did go through! But carrying around all that stress while trying not to squelch the excitement from others was tough. Little did I realize that what was coming my way in the next few weeks would be worse.

We had four days to do massive repairs and renovations to the homes on our new property, but decided it would save us time and thousands of dollars if we did all the work ourselves. Knowing this would put a major burden on our residents, we called a meeting for the Friday prior to moving in the residents from eleven different properties. Since the move had to take place the following weekend, we organized over two hundred volunteers to help with the move, which was done within a rainy forty-eight-hour period.

On Friday, the weekend before the move, about fifty residents and staff met at one of the homes where we enjoyed food and prayer together. Then I spoke to them regarding the transition, the importance of it, details of the renovations, and so on. But the most important thing I said that evening was, "The Devil doesn't like what we're doing. He will try to derail One Eighty, our leadership, and our residents. But we will put everything in God's hands."

And I was right.

The next ten days were some of the hardest days I've had in ministry. The battle began again with the city where the physical and mental health of our staff came under attack. The spiritual attacks and emotional draining we experienced were worse than any other time. Things were happening each day that were so bizarre I can't even describe them.

After about ten days of this, I decided to meet with all our residents in one of our recently acquired facilities. I asked them, "Besides me, has anyone else been under attack like no other time in your life?"

Everyone raised their hands.

"Remember, the one thing the Enemy can't rob us of is our joy," I said. "I've often heard, 'Is your glass half full or half empty?'" I continued. "That's a great question and a reminder to us. But in reality, *we* are in control of how much water we pour into the glass. God has given us the unique gift of being able to pour as much water as we want into that glass. His peace, love, grace, and joy is so abundant that we can fill that dang glass to overflowing, if we want."

I paused and looked around at all the faces. "Every morning when I wake up, I tell myself, *No matter what happens today—my joy will not be stolen.* Sadly, when we let situations steal our joy they're not just taking our joy, they're robbing the joy from others around us."

During those ten days, the Enemy tried everything he could to steal the joy from me, my family, and our organization. But he lost!

What good is a key if there's no lock? Of what use is the Holy Spirit and the power of Jesus—if we never need Him? James 1:2–4 says "Consider it pure joy, my brothers and sisters, whenever you face trials of many kinds, because you know that the testing of your faith produces perseverance. Let perseverance finish its work so that you may be mature and complete, not lacking anything" (NIV).

What or who is trying to steal your joy?

Just looking at a key doesn't unlock the door. In spiritual contexts, that's called religion, which is knowing God through a piece of paper without experiencing who He truly is. We didn't make it through those ten days of craziness just by talking about God. No, we prayed together, worshiped our Savior, and experienced Him throughout that journey.

When it comes to struggles we face in life, it's like our walk with Christ—you get better, or you get worse. There is no in between and there's no standing still. You either move forward or you move backward.

Paul writes in Romans 7 (paraphrased), "Why do I do the things I don't want to do?" Paul, one of the greatest heroes of the Bible, struggled just like you and I do, yet he recognized his weaknesses. Paul let God's glory shine through, and he let God's conviction bring correction. Paul then renewed his mind through the Spirit of God, not with the things of this world.

This is why it's important for us to see the big picture. Our little minds tend to focus on our current situation, circumstance, trouble, or temptation, but we never bother looking to see where that fits into the big picture.

Imagine a five- or six-year-old kid playing kick ball in the yard with you, the parent. The ball accidentally flies across the street and into the neighbor's yard. You live on a fairly busy road with cars whizzing by every few minutes. Your child's first reaction is to chase after the ball, while as the parent, you're left yelling, "Wait! Hold on! Wait for me! Watch out for the cars!" You see, the child sees the goal and nothing else, just sees the ball across the road and wants it. Children don't think about the oncoming traffic and the trouble or tragedy that's near.

Now compare that to your relationship with Christ. Waiting on God can be so tiring. We often ask, "Why isn't God getting me out of this situation? Why am I still stuck in jail? Why is my court case being continued yet again? Why am I not healthy yet?"

We're that child running after the ball (our goal), but we aren't seeing the big picture (the cars flying past). The whole time, God stands there saying, "Wait! Hold on! Wait for me! Watch out for the trouble ahead!"

In my life, it didn't matter whether I was sitting in a druggie's rundown home, meeting with an executive of a large business, or fighting for justice at a city council meeting, there were always battles, temptations, and struggles. They simply looked different.

And I finally realized that there's no special formula to overcome those things. Instead I have to decide every day to not fall into those traps. And I choose by actually using *the key* (Jesus), and staying focused on the big picture. Doing that unlocks the freedom I need access to in my life.

No, it doesn't mean I'm perfect. It doesn't mean that I don't have tough days and lose my joy at times. It just means that when my joy, faith, peace, and trust escape me, and when the waves of life seem too much, God's grace is always waiting for me. And His grace is waiting for you too. You just have to take it.

# Reflections from the Other Side of Society
### (Letter from a current inmate)

Dear Iva,

Hey, Princess, how are you? I'm having a bit of a hard time at the moment. . . .

As long as I live on this earth, baby girl, and look back, I've found an evident truth in this: I have the power to believe. It's when we lose this power that we lose hope. As a child, this is the strongest, but it grows harder to maintain as we grow up. Never lose this, my love, always believe.

What we believe in is important. All the signs and signals carry a person who believes to accomplish and reach their hopes and dreams. Believe and follow after the truth. The biggest enemy is time because we will often be tested against every hour, minute, and second.

We will be convinced that our dreams are impossible, that they will never come true. But know, my dear, anything becomes possible if we are patient enough to let ourselves be guided by our belief.

That's why I write continually, *always keep God close*. If you would like to know how one gets to point A or point B, it's all under the watchful eye of God. If there is a door one must enter, my love, that door is Jesus Christ. I will always point you to Jesus, my love, but I will never push you.

It's just that I've been lost and I sought answers. I've been broken, scared, and in deep darkness, but through Jesus, I found light, love, peace, and a sense of joy. All this I share with you comes from my power to believe. It's from my heart. You're my wonderful child and I don't want to see you go through the pain and suffering that comes from failed expectations by believing something false. But at the same time, I hope you know where to turn when and if it happens.

Let no one take away your belief. Not even time.

From my heart to yours,

Your father

## Interaction Map

1. List some other areas of your life in which you need the key.

2. What is going on in your life now that keeps you struggling to see the big picture?

# 6

# Maintaining Your Key:

## Keeping Freedom Once You Have It

Due to the large amount of acid, cocaine, alcohol, and pills I digested over the years my memory is shady, at best. There isn't much I can really remember clearly about my childhood. However, for some reason I can recall this one instance like it was yesterday.

One snowy day, my mother and I were on 55th Avenue, heading home from basketball practice. We lived on a farm about ten minutes from our small town. I was in the backseat when, suddenly, I heard my mom scream! We hit a patch of ice and within seconds, which felt like an eternity, we were in the ditch.

The reason I remember that is because it was like everything was in slow motion. Mom tried desperately to regain control of the car, but it seemed the harder she steered, the more out of control the car became.

I bet you've had one of those moments before—the more you try to take control of the steering wheel of life, the more out of control you feel. Then one day you wake up and realize you're in a ditch. It feels like depression, addiction, and anxiety won again.

I've had many of those moments in my life and can't count the times I've told myself, "Okay, it's a new day! Starting fresh. Not doing this stuff again!" Then the next day I find myself again saying the same thing because I didn't even make it through yesterday morning. Eventually, I got tired of making that promise and disappointing myself over and over. And since I felt that I was disappointing God, I just quit.

And it doesn't matter if it's sugar, drugs, alcohol, gambling, eating, pornography, and the list keeps going. During my struggles, I truly meant it when I woke up and told myself it was a new day. I wanted to quit my addiction and change my life. But I felt like my freedom window was so freaking small that it just gave me enough time to be disappointed once more.

So the million-dollar question is: how do you keep that freedom once you have it?

> But I felt like my freedom window was so freaking small that it just gave me enough time to be disappointed once more.

The first thing is to realize that we will never be perfect, and that's why we have God's grace. I've always heard, "You can't keep a bird from flying over your head, but you can keep it from landing on it." Temptation will come, just like the birds flying overhead.

Sadly, temptations, struggles, anxiety, and stress, are all part of life, and at times, we may succumb to them. But there are things we can put into place that help us battle them on a daily basis.

I wish I could tell you that you will live a happy and perfect life, with no more struggles or worries, but I'd be lying to you. And wouldn't it be boring and mind-numbing if you never ran into a problem? Your mind would never grow. But this life is full of ups and downs and highs and lows. Just how high your highs will be is determined on how you act when you're in a season of drought.

I mentioned earlier that I grew up on a farm. Hunting, fishing, and farming were part of our lifestyle. I learned to drive a tractor before I learned to drive a truck.

While in high school, I was sent home one day on an indefinite suspension. Of course, my parents were pretty upset, so they hooked me up with my Uncle Kim, who tended the family farm. I'll never forget those next few days because nearly every minute that the sun was up . . . I was in the field planting corn—by hand.

Let's just say, I learned a lot about corn. A kernel of corn is planted as a seed, which then grows into a stalk. During its short lifetime, it gets water from the rain. But when there's no rain, the cornstalk must get water from another source. So in a time of drought, its roots grow deeper searching for water.

The interesting fact is that this actually serves two purposes. One, to get water so it can grow. But two, when a storm comes and winds blow, its roots are so deep and strong because of its search for water, it can withstand the elements. Which in turn, produces what God intended all along.

That's your life.

When you're in a time of drought, don't give up, just dig deeper like that cornstalk. Because those moments will give you the endurance and strength to withstand future storms where you feel out of control, just like my mom's car that wintry day on 55th Avenue.

When the storms of life come, when temptations arise, and when your life spins out of control, your roots will be deep enough to withstand the tempest. And you will produce what God has called you for. Once you've been to the bottom, you have more appreciation for the ride to the top.

No matter how painful the situation is, you'll find peace in knowing that someway, somehow, God is in the middle and still in control. But in order to accomplish that goal, your relationship with Christ must go beyond the emotional moments in life.

If you want to really keep those moments of freedom you have experienced and defeat those temptations, you have to start with accountability.

Between the time I accepted Christ and when I met my beautiful, amazing wife, Brook, I spent an excruciating three years being single. Going from a sexually active lifestyle to a life of none, there were plenty of moments when temptation reared its head. By no means, did I pass with flying colors, however, outside of God's grace, accountability was the only thing that helped me get through this time.

Accountability was there to remind me that when it came to the opposite sex, I would rather have nobody instead of a wrong somebody. There were moments when accountability wasn't friendly either. And I came to the realization that rebuke isn't necessarily a bad thing. In my opinion, accountability is one of the single most important things you need when you're desperately seeking to stay within the freedom you've found.

However, no accountability is better than bad account-ability. I've discipled and been part of many people's lives who scream that they have accountability. But in all reality, they just have a friend. Accountability means having a person who will check your phone while at lunch. It means having a person who will call you to the carpet when your attitude toward your spouse is selfish. Accountability is having that person who will ask what you read in the Bible today.

This is the person who will ask, "Why'd you spend that extra ten dollars on a hat when I know you're struggling to pay your rent?"

During those three years of being single, my accountability partner didn't let me go to the mall alone. Not because I might check out the girls at Victoria's Secret, but that I would look for affirmation from others who might check me out. He even made me take a different way back to the recovery home I was running at the time, since it was on a busy road that followed a park on the river, overloaded with girls working on their tan in the summer months.

Yeah, it meant an extra fifteen minutes across town to avoid the temptation. But if it wasn't for that accountability, I'm not sure where I would be today.

Many people want to draw a line and ask, "How close can I get to that line without crossing over?"

I say, If you're asking that question you're already too close. Your goal is to keep as far away from that line as possible. Go ahead and draw the line, but don't use it as an excuse to flirt with sin and get close to the edge.

As a kid, one of my favorite things was playing in my dad's tackle box. I absolutely loved it . . . until I got snagged by a hook. If earth is the water and we are the fish, then Satan is the hook and temptation is our bait.

Temptation doesn't come with a big sign, "Come get me, I'm sin." Temptation comes in forms we least expect, inviting and attractive. As a child, I use to love playing in my dad's tackle box. A few times thought while playing with the attractive lures, I would get snagged on the hook that was hidden. I never saw the hook, just the cool-looking bait and lure.

And accountability is what gives us a different perspective and reminds us that the hook is hidden by the bait and lure.

Look at this from another perspective. Think about taking your child to the doctor to receive a shot. That's easily one of the most painful experiences you'll have as a parent. You see, a three-year-old getting a shot in the arm doesn't realize the importance of it. For me, the worst thing was knowing that there was a possibility that my son, Tannen, was thinking, "Why is my dad letting this happen?"

Tannen has no perspective on the situation in that moment. And sometimes I feel like a three-year-old when I'm going through something painful. I ask, *God, Father, why would You let this happen?"*

My Dad's response may not be verbal but I think His answer is found in the simple fact that He allows me to experience the difficulties. Read Hebrews 11:35–39 where it talks about some who trusted God were tortured and beaten, but received God's approval because of their faith. So instead of asking, *"Why? Why did You let this happen to me?"* you should say, *"Why not me? Thank You, Lord, that You promised to never leave me, and that You intercede on my behalf to the Father during the times of pain."*

God doesn't necessarily give us the answer; we won't truly know why until we meet Him one day. And once we meet Him, we probably won't care.

Recently I was reading an article on Facebook from the *Chicago Tribune* regarding Pope Francis and how he responded to, "Why do children suffer so much?" Here is an excerpt from that article:

The pope ditched his prepared remarks and spoke off the cuff in his native Spanish to respond to 12-year-old Glyzelle Palomar, who wept as she asked Francis why children suffer so much. Palomar, a former street child rescued by a church-run foundation, told him of children who are abandoned or neglected by their parents and end up on the streets using drugs or in prostitution.

"Why is God allowing something like this to happen, even to innocent children?" Palomar asked through tears. "And why are there so few who are helping us?"

A visibly moved Francis said he had no answer. "Only when we are able to cry are we able to come close to responding to your question," he said.

"Those on the margins cry. Those who have fallen by the wayside cry. Those who are discarded cry," the pope said. "But those who are living a life that is more or less without need, we don't know how to cry."

And he added: "There are some realities that you can only see through eyes that have been cleansed by tears."

Sometimes not knowing the answer to a question or a problem can be a good thing. It creates a dependency on something beyond our control. Think about when you were in school, if you didn't know an answer to a question on your homework, you either asked the teacher or you started doing research to find that answer. In other words, in that moment, you were dependent on someone else, not yourself.

God places us in situations in our life, where we may not know the answer, and it's in those moments He is calling us to Himself. I wish there was a secret trick, magic formula, or a hack that will help you maintain your freedom. But in all reality, it comes down to growing in times of drought, cultivating accountability, and learning to cry and trust God in the moments that simply don't make sense to us.

## *Reflections from the Other Side of Society*
(Poems from a current inmate)

### A Better Way

We are trapped in this world and this world won't give in. Truly deceived when Eve ate the fruit skin. Destined to die by this body that my soul is cocooned in. I am weakened by these demons and my vine is fruitless. Hesitation brings me closer to ruin. My vices are relentless and resistance is useless. Transfigured in His likeness and newness, He opens my eyes with His mercy, which provides a way to navigate these nautical lines while I grow in faith and meditate on my path in life.

Realize the darkness seeks the sunshine and in due time God repairs and heals our lives. These puddles will get deep, harder in line to keep our feet. But fear not, our Shepherd can see there are lions among His sheep, false hope and corrupt beliefs. If you sleep, the beast will feed on your confidence, but in defeat we find courage to carry on. Outstretch your hands and form a bond that can't be broken because of love. In the Word it's spoken of, a better way with promise of . . .

### The Looking Glass

Through the looking glass we perceive our own truth to be true. For it is approval that we seek, we desire to be used. We become the only thing that matters, just look at the contrast, we have adapted to the circumstances walking like a sociopath. Taking the road better known for leaving people all alone to see the fact of a reflection staring back. It reflects the sadness behind the eyes of the man you're looking at. We heave pebbles in the pond so the ripples can be seen. Now our view is askew and the truth is deceit.

The page we can change but the picture is the same. If I can grasp what it takes then my life will be saved.

The key is in the renewal of recycled goods made brand new yet revamped, like elemental coal from the earth is a diamond pressed and stamped. The re-invention of attention in the intentions of man subconsciously speaking clearly and there's no turning back.

## Interaction Map

1. Share an area of your life in which you've gained freedom and victory.

2. Share a time in your life where "drought" set in.

3. Think about your accountability person. Do you feel you have adequate accountability? If not, what should you do about it?

4. What are you facing or have faced that made you question, "Why is/has this happened?"

# Part 3:

Your Catalyst: The key doesn't just unlock your jail cell, it opens your dreams and destinies. Your story soon becomes the catalyst for your purpose in life.

# 7

# Discovering Your Catalyst:

## The Thing that Will Take You to the Next Level

While sitting in cell 121, I grew weary of watching men and women, who said they wanted to change their life, come back to the same dirty, dingy jail just months, or even weeks after being released. I knew when I was released that I had an amazing family and church home to go to. But not every guy or girl that I was in jail with had that same opportunity. The fact is, it's hard to get clean when you're in a mud puddle.

I love my son's puppy, Barnaby. He is a twelve-week-old Labrador and Golden Retriever mix. The other day for fifteen minutes, I watched that puppy try licking the mud off his legs and belly. The comical thing about it—he was sitting in a mud puddle the whole time.

> it's hard to get clean when you're in a mud puddle.

How many of us, like Barnaby, try to get our lives cleaned up, yet the environment we're doing it in isn't healthy? It would be like someone trying to eat healthier while working in the fast food industry and getting free food. Or someone wanting to quit drinking, but they're a bartender.

In cell 121, after watching these men, I knew what God was calling me to do. I needed, wanted, and was born to create a safe environment and atmosphere for men and women who truly wanted to change their life. I spent nearly the next year of my life in jail, not watching TV or playing games every day, but planning and creating what we now know as One Eighty.

Cell 121 was more than just my saving grace. It was the catalyst for what God was calling me to do for the rest of my life. All the drugs, parties, drinking, immorality, pain from losing friends, and the heartbreak of returning to jail all led to the calling God had in my life.

What have you faced that tried to take you out? If you surrender that thing to Christ and are open to what He can do in your life, there's a good chance that the thing the Devil meant to take you out will become the launching pad for the rest of your life and the vision God gives you.

Growing up in a small country church, I never heard the word *vision* in the context of a plan or an idea. Needless to say, I was very confused when I first heard *vision* or *God's calling*. But as God quickly worked on my heart, not only in cell 121 but after as well, vision developed into much more for me.

Over the years, I've studied exactly what a vision is, and here is how I would define it:

Visions are born in the soul of a person consumed with the tension of what is, and what could be, and is formed in the hearts of those who are dissatisfied with the status quo. It begins with the inability to accept things the way they are.

A vision is a preferred future and it demands change.

A vision hinges on someone's will to champion a cause and it will only become a reality if someone puts their neck on the line.

A vision requires the hearts and minds of men and women to wander outside the artificial boundaries of the world's thinking.

A visionary is someone who puts action to an idea.

But a dreamer is simply someone who has great plans but never sees them out. Dreamers dream about something being changed, and visionaries envision themselves being the change. A dreamer thinks about how something could be, and a visionary tries to forget how things look currently.

A visionary is often driven by a burden. A dreamer is driven by a passion. Both by themselves are not bad things. But passions come and go. And a burden doesn't leave, continuing to hurt until you lighten the load with action.

Early in my nonprofit career, there were so many times I wanted to throw in the towel. If I'd been fueled by passion, I would have. But it was a burden, and I knew it would hurt if I quit.

In the late 1800's, the US Government and War Department contracted with a man by the name of Samuel Pierpont Langley. Langley was a professor, scientist, and head of the Smithsonian Institute, and was paid over $1 million in US currency. His mission was to develop the first manned aircraft. He was well connected and hired the best minds. All the newspapers followed the story.

Want to know why you never heard of him? It's because of two men, the Wright brothers. They had a vision, a burden, but no college education. Their small-town bicycle shop became their funding source and before Langley could set flight, the Wright brothers accomplished the once thought impossible task.

The difference between Langley and the Wright brothers was very simple. The Wright brothers were driven by a cause, a purpose, and a belief that if they could figure this out it would change the world for the better. Their burden drew others who believed in their dream.

The day the Wright brothers took flight . . . Langley quit.

I wish I could tell you that burdens only come out of a desire that God puts in your heart. But in reality, burdens oftentimes come from pain and hurt.

When I was a teenager, I had a close friend named Evan. Evan and I played baseball together. We were always on the same team and we shared the same passion. Evan was tall, I was short, but we made a great duo. He pitched and I caught. He hit homers and, well, I usually walked.

One evening, after years of friendship, my mom picked me up from school and told me that Evan had passed away. I was crushed and felt numb and dead on the inside. But I refused to show any emotion on the outside, until his visitation was over.

On the way home from the funeral parlor, sitting next to my brother, I broke down in the back of my parents' SUV.

"Why, God?" I questioned. "Evan was the first friend I ever felt close to and You took him away from me." And it took a long time to get over that trauma.

Ever since Evan's death, I had trouble getting close to anyone. But one day, I became involved in the Civil War Reenactments. During that time, I met Frank and Jesse, two men who became father figures to me. I talked to these men almost daily and they taught me to train and ride horses. For the first time since Evan's death, I felt close to other guys.

Within five years, both those men were taken from me. One died from cancer, the other completely stopped talking to me, for some unknown reason. I still find myself calling him, hoping someday he'll answer.

But once again, I blamed God. "Why would You let everyone I get close to disappear? Am I not supposed to ever have friends?"

Over time, things become engrained in our lives, and for years, I believed that if I got close to someone they would either let me down or die. Because of that, I lived a life of jumping from friend to friend, but never having a really close or best friend.

I went from girl to girl, and if one got too close, I got rid of her and moved on. I sabotaged any relationship that was getting too close, all because of the fear that I learned through life's experiences.

Looking back, I now see that I can get close to someone without getting hurt. God allowed those things to happen to me and used them to mold me into who I am today. Of course, I wish those things had never happened, but they did. And if you took them away from my story, I wouldn't be the man I am today, nor have a burden for the people I strive to serve. I wish Evan hadn't died, I wish Jesse hadn't died, and God knows, I wish Frank hadn't just exited my life. But they did.

It took me years to process that hurt and pain. And finally I realized that God used Evan, Frank, and Jesse to make a big impact in my life so I can make a big impact on others.

God will turn your mess into a message. He has a unique way of taking your pain, using it as a megaphone to impact the world, and somehow your suffering becomes a servant to your message, which is amplified to others.

Those things in life that were designed to take you out, end up becoming the catalyst for what you were created to do.

## *Reflections from the Other Side of Society*
(Letter from a current inmate)

Iva,

Hey, Love Bug, how goes it? I prayed for your protection today. I was sitting in parenting class thinking about the people you may be around while I am gone. I love you and miss you very much.

My parenting class is going well. I'm learning methods of giving instructions, effective communication skills, teaching rules and rewards. I plan on learning these things and applying them to our relationship someday.

My favorite thing I've learned is giving you freedom to explore and in explaining what things are to you. I am also excited to see you explore creativity. I will protect you from danger and I will protect your freedom. I pray you get to see the dad I can be.

Because I've made God my first love I can now truly love you, and I have the capacity to love others—even myself. One day, I hope you do too.

Love,
Dad

## Interaction Map

1. My catalyst was cell 121. What's yours?

2. Growing up, what did you want to be as an adult? And why?

3. What is your dream and vision for your life now?

# 8

# Understanding Your Catalyst:

## Creating an Action Plan for that Dream to Become Reality

I've learned that when God gives you a vision, dream, or idea the most important thing is to give it back to Him. I've watched many great people with tremendous ideas take a vision from God and act like it was theirs. They forget the source of all good, creativity, and burdens.

Early in my ministry career, I began saying a simple prayer that enabled me to make it through some of my pain:

*God, thank You for entrusting me with this vision, dream, and burden. Father, it's Yours. Do with it as You want.*

I was hired by a local organization (not One Eighty) as the Men's Home Director and my goal was to create a men's facility out of nothing. Then one day, with no warning, my boss called me and said, "Rusty, I need you to gather together all the guys living in that home. Have everyone sit around the kitchen table, including yourself, and I'll be there soon."

After a few minutes of waiting patiently, my boss walked in, followed by a few board members and a couple of other people. She handed me a letter and said, "Please read this aloud to everyone."

As I finished the first paragraph I realized I was reading my letter of termination. After just nine months on the job, I was fired. But being fired wasn't what hurt the most, it was the fact that I had to read it out loud to the very guys I was in charge of leading.

The moments following the reading didn't get any better. My then ex-boss said, "You are required to leave the property immediately. However, you may have twenty-four hours to remove any personal belongings."

I felt heat climb up my neck and race to the top of my head. My heart starting beating so fast it felt like it would pop out of my chest. I clenched my fists to keep from hitting something. My vision had just been kidnapped! I'd worked so hard to build this dream, investing sixty, sometimes seventy hours a week into it. I had even taken a 70 percent cut in pay. This was my home! My future! And in one instant—it was gone.

The letter stated I was fired, ". . . for leaving the house phone sitting out on the weekends where the guys were able to use it."

On weekends, I stayed at my parents' home and spent time with my son. I knew it was against the rules to leave the phone where the men had access to it. But since the residents weren't allowed to have cell phones, I felt they needed to have a phone available in case of emergency.

After a lot of prayer and a few meetings, I was able to move back into the house. But that episode created a real bond between me and the men I was serving. That bond grew even stronger between us as we realized that we were like being in a boat in the ocean, with no idea of our destination, and quickly running out of supplies we desperately needed for the journey.

So I, my leadership team, and the current residents started our own ministry (prematurely, I might add, but it was the only option I saw at the time). One Eighty was born in July of 2009, out of the heartbreak from that situation. And this was just the beginning of God's wonderful divine plan that He had in store for One Eighty.

I've never been afraid to chase after my dreams, even in the midst of turmoil and heartbreak. And starting One Eighty with only five hundred dollars in my pocket, was no different.

My highest level of education is graduation from an alternative high school. Yet I was smart enough to know at the onset that in order to be successful and to truly grow One Eighty, I had to surround myself with men and women who had wisdom in areas that I didn't have yet at age twenty-one.

One Eighty started with twelve of us sitting around a table in the kitchen of a member's home. Many of those people are still with us today, eight years later. We spent countless hours praying, dreaming, and planning. We shed tears, blood, and sweat together building a model that we truly felt would change how this world sees rehabilitation. We'd all dreamed this would happen, but now that the dream was becoming a reality, I found myself with an unquenchable thirst to do more. Although I constantly have to ride the line and ask, "For whose glory are we doing this?"

And I believe that as long as we live in that tension, continually asking the question, and reaffirming that we're doing it for God's glory, we will always be in a good place.

Even though this team and I experienced some amazing mountain tops, we've also gone through some deep and dark valleys. And one of those valleys came about because we asked ourselves, "Why are we doing this?"

There was no question, in my early years of ministry, that I felt I had failed and let that group down. Our home was designed to house men who wanted to change their life, over a long period of time. But it soon became a revolving door of guys who really had no interest in being there.

One day, I came home to a resident sitting on the patio drinking a beer. Baffled, I asked, "What in the world are you doing?"

"Drinking."

I stared at him in amazement. "You do realize that this is a sober living environment? You're here to stop drinking."

"Yeah," he quickly replied, "but I decided I didn't want to quit. By the way, do you have a dollar? I need one more and I'll be good."

Sadly, in the early days this was more than a rare occurrence. Before long, I felt more and more like a failure. Our launch team revisited how we were doing our ministry. We philosophically took on a new approach—Quality over Quantity. Instead of jamming twelve guys into a four-bedroom home, who didn't want to change, we decided we'd rather have only one guy living in a four-bedroom home, who truly wanted to change.

Over time, we found a formula that worked and soon we added another guy who truly wanted to change. Then another . . .

I wish I could tell you that was the end of the tough moments for One Eighty. But a few years later, I found myself facing another valley and learned one more hard lesson.

For years, I worked side by side with some of the most amazing couples I've ever known. One couple in particular, became two of my closest friends. They're the type of people that you could eat three meals a day with them and still miss them when you went home at the end of the day. They understood me, what I was thinking, my vision, and my heart.

But a few years into One Eighty, I made one of the biggest mistakes of my life. As a leader, I allowed church politics and outside influences to creep into my heart. It all came to a head when these two friends made a few bad decisions. It wasn't anything we couldn't have worked through, but because of those outside influences that crept in, it led to me approaching them about terminating their employment.

Now I could justify my decision on paper, but in a ministry of grace and love, when I look back I realize that I made a premature decision.

One of the more difficult moments of my life was walking down this hallway—only about twenty yards long, but that day it felt like two thousand yards long. However, what happened after I made that incredibly long walk down the tan colored hallway not only changed One Eighty, but my style of leadership forever.

I entered the empty room we were to meet in, white walls, four chairs, and a small table. *Yes! They're not here so I don't have to do this right now.* As soon as that thought crossed my mind—in they walked. Not only were they my best friends, they were two of the first three employees I'd ever had. And in my entire life I had never let anyone go.

Things started off awkwardly because they already had an idea of what was going to happen, were probably a little numb and wondering where this was coming from.

After all, these were the people who had dreamed with me for countless hours on how we were going to change the world. And that was about to change in a ten-minute conversation.

I wish I could tell you it went smoothly and I was a strong leader during that meeting. But I wasn't. I cried. And cried. Then cried some more. I'd written out what I was going to say, but I couldn't read more than five words without hyperventilating.

The couple asked if they could read the paper, but my dad taught me that as a man and a leader, the buck stopped with me, so I fought off the temptation to have them read it out loud. I finally took a deep breath and did my best to go over the needed documents.

At the end of the meeting when I handed them the paper to sign, I noticed that it was drenched with my tears. And if I could go back and do that day over, I would.

Growing up, I worked on a ranch and farm, training horses. I loved riding horses, but I learned from watching John Wayne movies that if I was thrown off, I dusted off my pants, hopped back up into the saddle again, and rode off. And the day after my friends had left, I felt like I'd just been thrown from a horse. But I couldn't stay down, I had to dust myself off, saddle up, learn from my mistakes, and ride on. I had to grow a backbone and stand by what I felt was the right decision.

That moment could have locked me in an emotional jail. But instead, God used it as a catalyst to shape the identity of One Eighty and the environment that we strive to create for our leaders while strengthening my leadership. But I had the choice of locking myself in a jail or launching myself into the next level of my leadership.

Looking back, the right choice was clear. Yet in that moment, I was in a battle between feeling sorry for myself, full of regret, anger, and doubt, and doing what John Wayne taught me—getting back into the saddle and riding on.

I'm confident that the experience I had that day not only changed me, but the One Eighty for the better. God took the shattered pieces I'd created with my bad leadership and turned them into the catalyst of how to do my ministry for the rest of my life. During those times in my life, I remind myself—*all great things are made by not so great times.*

> I had the choice of locking myself in a jail or launching myself into the next level of my leadership.

War, drought, disease, murder, rape, addiction, greed, theft, any type of sin, and death on a cross doesn't sound like great times to me. However, those not so great times produced the number one best-selling book of all times, the Bible.

There are always birthing pains before a child is born. It's hard, it sucks, and it's painful (so I hear), but they must happen in order for each one of us to be born. In your life now, you might be in some pain, but when you make it through the agony, God will show you the wonderful creation that results.

I didn't enjoy sitting in jail. I hated being fired. I detested feeling that I failed our team on how we were doing ministry. I regret seeing two great staff members leave because of my lack of leadership. But one of the great things about this story—it doesn't end there!

One of the amazing things about God is that when a crisis happens, He allows us freedom, even though He always maintains control. Just as Jesus and Barabbas were taken in front of the crowd to decide their fate, God remained in control. In Mark 15, we read that the crowd began to cry, "Free Barabbas and crucify Jesus!"

You see, this didn't make sense because Barabbas was the known criminal and Jesus was simply a religious radical. God didn't manipulate the words coming out of the mobs' mouths that day from "Free Barabbas" to "Free Jesus," although He definitely could have done so. He let things play out according to Scripture, letting the decisions and choices happen, but He stayed control.

I wish I had a creative action plan for you to follow step by step, but I don't. However, the most important things I learned through my experiences are pretty simple.

*Give your dream back to God.*

*Be humble enough to surround yourself with people who are strong where you are weak.*

*Don't be afraid to re-visit your dream in order to improve it.*

*Never quit, even when it seems like the bottom has fallen out and your dream has vanished.*

If you follow these four principles within whatever God has you to do, there is no question in my mind that you will succeed.

## *Reflections from the Other Side of Society*
### (Poems from a current inmate)

**Love**

If love is a feeling, then pain is equivalent to an ugly step-child of an abusive stepparent. We reel from the pain and horror we face when we reach for our love and our love turns to dust. Questions fill gaps as life becomes scripted, relationships are damaged like rafts that have drifted. Till finally we fall and through grace we are changed. We open our eyes to assess the extent of our pain.

Learning to love myself is a feeling so foreign. My thoughts lead to shame like a house that's unsorted. A change in the process, the picture distorted. But that house is my home and that mess is my life, so the work must be done so the love I can find. Time becomes precious as love takes a hold, divinely aligned, mind, body, and soul, with my feet on the ground and my world on its axis. I thank God for His Word when the world is the blackest. Proudly I know in Him we are, for I'm forged through my experience of pain and of love.

Love conquers all because love is a giant defeating the hate. Love is defiant, while understanding our pain. Love nurtures the righteous and is the point of living and dying.

**The Process**

I found pieces to the puzzle, and I was perplexed they didn't fit. Feeling lost in this life, I think my compass needs fixed. With a sword in my hand with a needle-razor tip, I plunge forward through the darkness, inching closer to the pit. I realize that I'm flawed from the hate that I'm in. And I'm on the edge of dying 'cause my will has been stripped. Long ago I decided there's no reason to obey now. I'm ahead of myself and being carried away. As if my soul checked out but my body remains, my circumstances circumvent and then my conscience complains. I'm afraid of the dark but the darkness remains. Desperately I'm in need of some hope, the very reason for trying. A Savior of grace to start the rewinding, submerged in His Word I am then unbinding. I fell on my knees and said, "Thanks for the impeccable timing."

I stand fast in the promise for the future tomorrow, comfortable in the contact and repaying what I borrowed. Taking note of His masterpiece like the stroke of one's art, His voice I now hear like the pluck of His harp. Thank God for the extractions of my soul from the world—the process that turned sand into beautiful pearls.

## Interaction Map

1. Do you really believe that the dream you identified in chapter 7 can become a reality? Why or why not?

2. What's holding you back from accomplishing that dream?

3. Have you given your dream back to God? If not, take a minute and do so now.

4. What are some hiccups and imperfections that have kept you from achieving the dream? And what steps can you take to eliminate them?

# 9

## Maintaining Your Catalyst:

### Living Your Dream

People oftentimes overcomplicate what it means to live their dream and what they should do with their life. It's actually a pretty simple concept. Your job is to show the world what Jesus would look like in your situation. What would Jesus look like if He was a roofer, an inmate, a construction worker, a carpet-layer, a lawyer, a congressman, and so on? This is why you were created. There's a massive story going on—the story of God. And even if you don't realize it, you're part of it. Part of living your dream is being open to what God is calling you to do, and it often takes a step of faith to be obedient in that dream.

I remember the days I worked as a roofer, yet I knew that God was going to call me to something different. But in order to achieve that "something different," I had to be faithful in what God had me doing currently. The same is true for today.

As One Eighty continues to grow, I've learned that if I don't grow as well, one of two things will happen. Either the ministry will outgrow my leadership and someday the board of directors will replace me, or my lack of growth will prohibit the growth of One Eighty. As I continue to challenge myself, the number one thing I've learned about leadership is that my job as a leader isn't necessarily to be liked. Of course, I want people to like me, but it can't be my overarching goal.

My job as a leader is to make hard decisions, even when they aren't popular. I've learned that the right decision is usually the hardest one—proven to be a great test when I make decisions.

Without question, throughout the last six years of One Eighty I made some bad decisions. I didn't always lead in the best way. I let anger get the best of me, I let my emotions rule my convictions, and I failed miserably at times. But God's grace always trumps our lack of judgment and poor decision-making.

As a leader, in order to create a healthy environment, it's important to understand that your vision will thrive in a state of unity, but die among division. You don't guide an organization with policies and procedures, but with principles.

> You don't guide an organization with policies and procedures, but with principles.

Your policies and procedures simply assist in implanting your principles.

Leadership is more than just leading a meeting or using fancy words. Leading is serving those on your team and becoming their number one fan. The difference between leadership and management is that management maintains the standard and flow of the work or ministry, while leadership elevates it.

As leaders, we often make decisions that are uncomfortable and tremendously hard, and for that we receive criticism, complaints, and accusations. I believe this is why Jesus spoke firmly about trusting those in authority. If you're being led, do your leader a favor and be slow to jump to unpleasant conclusions and quick to offer encouragement.

It doesn't mean that conflict and disagreement won't happen, but a healthy outcome is possible if there is a mutual respect for the purity of each other's motives. If your team truly believes that everyone has the right motives and are on the same page, it makes disagreeing much harder.

You won't be perfect, and you will fall at times, but it's not whether we fall, it's who we fall *on* that makes the difference. As a leader, one of the areas that's easy to fail in, is trusting God when disappointment happens.

Have you ever invested a great amount of time, energy, and resources into something or someone only to be disappointed? For years, I watched residents in our program that we devoted countless hours and dollars to, walk away from it all, and that can be quite a shock. You hurt for them, are disappointed, heartbroken, and question yourself, "Could I have done something differently?"

So what do you do when that happens? You get back up and fight for the next one. But in order to do that you have to realize that life isn't a party boat—it's a battleship. You won the fight on the back of a God who came to this earth and died for you. But you must carry out that victory, because the only way you'll lose is if you give up.

Early in my ministry, I was reminded of this in a harsh way. I lived in our Men's Recovery Facility for four years, due to accountability and the budget. I felt that was the best choice for myself and for our organization. I had many great experiences during this time, while others weren't so great. But I wouldn't trade those days for anything.

One of the not so great memories came from a guy I'll call Richard, who lived there for nearly a year. Richard, a past heroin addict in his twenties, lost his mom at a young age. But he decided he wanted to go back to school, so he enrolled in college. And within a year, he earned a bachelor's degree in business administration, and ended up in a position of management.

Richard was the perfect poster boy for One Eighty. Then one dreadful day, another staff member and I came home to find Richard on our kitchen floor, barely alive, overdosed on heroin. Although Richard eventually recovered in a hospital, sadly, it was the last time One Eighty saw him.

Just like with Richard, while living your dream, you'll have moments of, "I can't do this anymore," or "Why do I do this?" That's when you have to depend on God to get you through.

Shortly after Richard's situation, I had a "Why do I do this?" moment. We rescued an eighteen-year-old I'll call Frank, from a house of prostitution. The woman running it was in her fifties and she took in runaways. In return for a place to stay she prostituted them and had them run drugs.

Frank was a good kid who had grown up in a horrible environment. After a few months of being in our program, Frank's life began to change drastically. He got a job, was rebuilding relationships with his family, was becoming part of the church, and everything was going in his favor.

One day Frank and I went grocery shopping, and when we got back to the house I began putting up what we'd bought. Suddenly, I heard Frank on the phone yelling at his mom. I looked over my shoulder to see exactly what was going on—in time to duck as the phone came flying by my head.

I knew Frank was upset and things wouldn't end well. I could hear Frank throwing stuff around in his room.

My cell phone was in my bedroom, which was the room next to his. I ran in and grabbed my phone, just as I felt Frank's hands on my shoulders.

Frank is a big, strong kid, while I'm only 5 foot 4 and less than 115 pounds. He spun me around and held a Sawzall to my throat. He said, "You better start praying because it's going to be the only thing that will save your life today."

So I took his advice . . . and prayed. I'll never forget the feeling of that Sawzall blade shoved to my throat, just below my jaw. I knew Frank was serious and the rage I saw in his eyes that day, well, I can't even put my feelings into words.

When I started praying out loud, Frank dropped the Sawzall and began weeping. We moved to the couch and he asked me to read Scripture passages to him. But when I got to Jeremiah 29:11, where God says (paraphrased), "I know the plans I have for you, good plans to give you a hope and a future," Frank flipped out again. He stormed into the kitchen and I could hear him going through the knife drawer. I knew it was time to leave.

I snuck out, locked myself in my car, and seconds later, Frank ran out of the house with a knife all the way through one wrist and another knife in his other hand. Frank then chased some junior high kids down the road, waving the knife. He fought a dad taking his kids to the park, and eventually barricaded himself in the house. The police finally raided the house and took Frank out on a stretcher. It seemed like there was blood all over the house. Cops were everywhere.

I'd managed to escape down the block and stood on a pier overlooking the Mississippi River. "Why do I do this?" I asked myself. Then I asked God, *Why do I do this?* Finally I said to myself, "I can't do this anymore."

I felt God tell me, *"I never gave up on you . . . why are you giving up on me?"*

As you venture on in life, you'll continue to battle the demons of your past, the struggles, addictions, and hardships that try to steal your dream and keep it from becoming a reality. However, God never gives up on you . . . don't give up on him!

As your journey through life continues I want to encourage and challenge you to face and identify your jail.

> I felt God tell me, *"I never gave up on you . . . why are you giving up on me?"*

Once you know what your jail is, create a battle plan to overcome it. And don't be disappointed if your jail cell doesn't unlock immediately. You have to desperately seek the key that brings freedom and understand that the key unlocks other areas of your life as well.

And then create accountability—find someone who will hold you accountable, and will be there to help you keep your freedom once you experience it.

The last step is discover how your jail can become your catalyst. Create a plan of action for your dream to become a reality, and then simply live out the dream God has placed in your heart.

Following those steps led to the freedom that I live in today. It doesn't mean I'm struggle free, it simply means I have a God who is bigger than

> It doesn't mean I'm struggle free, it simply means I have a God who is bigger than my struggles.

my struggles. I truly believe that the steps I shared with you through this book will work in your life and lead you to the new you.

Welcome to your new life!

## *Reflections from the Other Side of Society*
(Letter from a current inmate)

Iva,

I have not heard your voice for some time now. I have no more phone calls left, I gave my last one to a person in need. I do hold dear every phone call when I get to hear your voice close to me and it's so precious. But it's also my duty to help those in need. I hope you can adopt this mindset also. I love you.

Daddy

## Interaction Map

1. Are you showing the world what Jesus would look like if he was in your occupation or position? If so, how are you doing it? If not, pray about it.

2. Do you see yourself as a leader? If so, why? If not, why?

3. What is your burden?

4. What are some of your passions?

5. Share one of your disappointments while chasing your dream.

# Closing

I want to close with a moment of vulnerability. I love coaching my son's baseball team. Not because he's an All-Star, even though he is. I love coaching it because without God I wouldn't be here and be part of his life. As I write this, Tannen is eight years old and he has two sets of parents.

The last few years, both sets of Tannen's parents have had the honor of being involved in coaching his teams. His stepdad and I coach on the field, and his mother and stepmom (my wife) help in the dugout and with the score board. At first we got some weird looks. And I'd be lying if I said it wasn't weird for me too, in the beginning.

The first few times I heard my son call another man Dad, it crushed me. At eight years old, out on the diamond, I heard him yell, "Hey, Dad."

I turned around—and saw him talking to his stepdad.

But when I look back on my life, I realize God used Tannen to change my life, before he was even born. Before Tannen and cell 121, I was an addicted, homeless bum, undeserving of a loving God and His miraculous grace.

I'm not supposed to be writing this book from my kitchen table, with my dog at my feet, my beautiful wife expecting, and a game to coach tonight, with my son playing first base. Without God, I'm supposed to be sitting in a prison in downstate Illinois.

My outlook on life is no longer, "This is unfair." Instead, I'm blessed to even be a part of God's story here on earth. And yeah, my son may call another man Dad, but he also calls my wife, Mom. Some kids don't even have one parent who loves them—Tannen has four.

It wasn't fun sitting in cell 121, seeing my name spread across the TV screens and newspapers, or waking up in abandoned cars, battling addiction, and getting used to my son calling another man Dad. But it was those things that were the catalyst to make me who I am and help with what I do today.

You see, we each have a jail cell. You may not be surrounded by iron bars, but if you're honest, you have your struggles, which oftentimes imprison you.

In life, things may not always work out the way you want them to. But when you sit back and realize that there is a loving God out there whose grace trumps your bad decisions, it gives you a new perspective on life.

The crazy thing about it . . . we all have the same key.

The key doesn't just unlock your jail cell, it unlocks your dreams and destinies. Your story soon becomes the catalyst for your purpose in life.

What's your jail cell?

Are you willing to let God be your key?

And are you ready to let your past become the catalyst for your destiny?

## *Reflections from the Other Side of Society*
(Letter from a current inmate)

Iva,

This is my right hand. You can put yours on mine if you want. One day soon you will be able to hold my hand if you want to. . . .

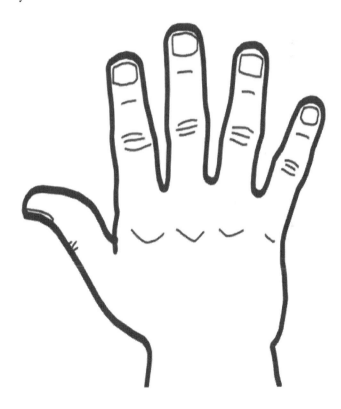

# About the Author

Rusty Boruff is Founder and Director of One Eighty, a faith-based nonprofit organization. The One Eighty vision was and is inspired by Rusty's personal life experiences. Though you might not think it upon first glance or encounter with Rusty, he was a drug addict, homeless, incarcerated, and eventually  unemployable. Through those experiences, Rusty experienced the love and support of real friends and family.

Sadly, though, he realized not everyone had what he had. Eventually Rusty bought a trailer with his savings and opened up a residential facility for men. Fast forward just six years and One Eighty now operates a nationally known program that includes three key areas: Prevent, Reach, and Develop. It's helped thousands overcome struggles in their life and has reached out to thousands of other kids who are at risk of taking the same road Rusty did.

Rusty also founded many businesses with One Eighty that are designed to be employment opportunities for those in their residential program.

Rusty has raised millions of dollars for the community, leads a volunteer force of hundreds, and is a highly sought after speaker and community leader. He was able to do all of this before his thirtieth birthday. However, if you ask him what his biggest accomplishment is, he would tell you it's being married to his beautiful wife, Brook, and raising their eight-year-old son, Tannen.

# We Are the Broken

In 2012, I received a phone call from Emmy- and Grammy-nominated actor, singer, and songwriter, Matthew West. At this time, Matthew West had a few number-one hits in the Christian music industry and was on his way to becoming a household name. During our conversation, Matthew shared with me that he'd been inspired by my story and penned a song called, "We Are the Broken."

This was the start of an amazing and continuing journey between Matthew and me. That song featured on his album, "Into The Light," which ignited his journey of being one of the most sought after and best-selling musicians of all time in the Christian industry. You can check out more of our relationship and the song by visiting my website: www.rustyboruff.com.

# Acknowledgments

This story was made possible only by a loving God and His infinite grace. I will forever be in debt to my parents, Rick and Lori, who never gave up on me; my brother, Rye, who protected our country overseas; my son, Tannen, who inspires me every day; and my wife, Brook, who puts up with my crazy personality and faults and is my biggest supporter. I love you.

I want to thank all the supporters, volunteers, and leaders at One Eighty and those we are able to serve through God's ministry. A special thank you to Traci and Ben, among others, who put countless hours into this book. A huge thank you to the Author Academy Elite team and our leader, Kary Oberbrunner. Also to my church family and my pastors, where I drew much of the inspiration to author this book. And to Cec Murphey, who has encouraged me in my writing and given me a scholarship to have this book published.

# Work Cited

Chapter 1
Jeremy Garvin, *Reflections from the Other Side of Society.*

Chapter 2
Ibid.
13 Foxtrot Forward Observer, www.goarmy.com, accessed

Chapter 3
Jeremy Garvin, *Reflections from the Other Side of Society,*

Chapter 4
Ibid.

Chapter 5
Ibid.
Americans with Disability Act, www.eeoc.gov., accessed
Federal Fair Housing Act, www.justice.gov.

Chapter 6
Jeremy Garvin, *Reflections from the Other Side of Society.*
*When Drought Comes*, Duane DeBoef. P. 130.
Pope Francis's remarks, *Chicago Tribune.*

Chapter 7
*Reflections from the Other Side of Society*, Jeremy Garvin.
Wright Brothers Story, Smithsonian Library; *Aviation Pioneer*, by William Baxter.

Chapter 8
*Reflections from the Other Side of Society*, Jeremy Garvin.

Chapter 9
*Reflections from the Other Side of Society*, Jeremy Garvin.

# JOIN THE MOVEMENT

## RUSTY BORUFF

INSPIRE PEOPLE · EQUIP DREAMS · IMPACT COMMUNITIES

Rusty is available to speak to your business, church, or organization!

## FOR ADDITIONAL RESOURCES

 www.rustyboruff.com

 www.facebook.com/rustyboruff

 www.twitter.com/rustyboruff

# Are you or a loved one going through a tough time?

**12:2** is a workbook resource that uses Rusty's story to help others walk through theirs. This is a great book for someone struggling with anything in their life. 12:2 has been used in many prisons, jails, and organizations across America.

"I got your book this morning and opened it up tonight to read it. It's not at all what thought. I was thinking I was going to read a life story, but after reading the first chapter I realize, like so many others in my family, I am an addict. My addiction is food and you acknowledged it as an addiction. So after I put the book down, I thought to myself, I should go get a bowl of ice cream or some chips. I got a glass of water instead." **-Michelle**

"I won your book at a drawing and decided to give it to my son who is an alcoholic. Not only did he read it, which was to my surprise, but he carries it with him wherever he goes and describes it as the only reason he is holding onto life." **— Marla**

# JOIN THE MOVEMENT

one eighty
PREVENT. REACH. DEVELOP.

For **additional resources** on
**One Eighty** and the programs offered visit:

www.oneeighty.org
www.facebook.com/180zone
www.twitter.com/180zone